MICHAEL CECCHETELLI

CROSSED KEYS

BIBLIOTHÈQUE ROUGE

MMXI

Published by Scarlet Imprint
under the *Bibliothèque Rouge* banner
Translation © Michael Cecchetelli, 2011
With additional notes by Peter Grey
& edited by Alkistis Dimech
Design by *fauxfaux*

ISBN 978-0-9567203-4-4
Printed and bound in the USA

CONTENTS

Preface & Introduction

The Black Dragon

The Infernal Forces Subject to Man

The Enchiridion of Pope Leo III

A rare gift & correspondence from His Serenity,
in the Vatican, to the Holy Emperor Charlemagne.

Notes to the *Black Dragon* & the *Enchiridion*

Dedicatio

PREFACE

HIS IS THE FIRST widely available
English language translation of
the classical grimoire known as *Le
Véritable Dragon Noir: Les Forces In-
fernales Soumises à l'Homme*, or *The
True Black Dragon: the Infernal Forces
Subject to Man*. Sharing spirits with
the *True Grimoire* and *Red Dragon*, as
well as some of the Elemental Kings from the *Goetia*, this
is a curious text which may illuminate these others in its
own peculiar black light. It is bound to a second translation, that of the *Enchiridion of Pope Leo III*, for reasons which
will become apparent, despite the seeming incongruity
of an infernal text pressing palms with a work of psalm
magic. As such the combined work bears the title of *Crossed
Keys*.

Before endeavoring to introduce this volume it be-
hooves me to spend a moment introducing myself in the
interests of assuring you that this book is the creation of
an active and practicing Magus and not an armchair or
theoretical magician. I set out on my path at age 15, primarily within the Golden Dawn system. While claiming to

i

have practiced magick from such a young age may sound to some a flight of fancy, I can assure you it was work of a most serious nature. My teacher was an Adept in the truest sense of the word. Not one of these new age astrally initiated internet adepts, but one who played the game in its original form. I studied with him until the age of 18, when I finally opened my first of the classical grimoires, the Mathers/Crowley *Goetia*. That book became the catalyst for my transformation. That was 13 years ago, and I have never looked back. I have made the magick of the grimoires and the Ancients my sole pursuit and to it I have remained faithful.

While I continue to study many magickal philosophies and systems, traditional evocation and grimoire magick have become my life's work, and in this field I have found great success. What separates me from any one of the thousands of others that make this claim is that due to a very unique set of circumstances I had four years of monastic existence wherein I had zero responsibilities, no obligations and absolutely nothing to do but read, study, theorize and practice magick. My entire life consisted of a 9 × 12 foot room where my sole possessions were a small bed, a toilet sink combination, an AM/FM walkman and a small desk. As you may have guessed, I'm referring to a prison. Maximum security federal prison. For nearly 4½ years, that cell was my entire world, and I was permitted to leave it only for a 15 minute daily shower and one hour of exercise three times a week. I was prohibited from making even the

standard prisoners' collect calls, and every piece of mail I
sent and received was photocopied and read before reach-
ing me or leaving the walls of the prison. I was believed
to hold the leadership role in what the bureau of prisons
considers a Security Threat Group, and I was segregated
because, quoting my classification report: *Inmate's presence
in a general population or less restrictive environment would pose
a threat to the safety and security of the orderly running of the institution and its staff.* I was, however, permitted access to
the prison chaplain and, through him, to order books via
any mail order company. I offer this glimpse into my life
not to convince the reader that I am some big, dark, scary
figure, but because this sentence, intended to punish me
for my transgressions of man's law, became the the means
by which my magickal development was facilitated, and,
indeed, expedited.

Consider if you will the scenario in which I found myself and how it differs from that of the modern Magus,
who, aside from his study and practice of magick, has to
simultaneously live a mundane life. I had absolutely no responsibilities, no obligations, no duty, no distraction from
wife or child, no TV, no junk food or other deterrents to
progress. My entire world was a 9 × 12 cement room.

I encourage each of you to sit a moment in contem-
plation of this. With 4½ years in this level of solitude,
having vast experience with lucid dreaming, astral travel
and magick, with nothing to keep you company but the
collected works of Aleister Crowley and copies of every

grimoire and magickal treatise you could find available by mail order or that you could convince the chaplain to print off the internet, and absolutely no distractions of any sort, to what heights (or depths) could your development reach?

Under those exact conditions, using candles carved out of bars of soap, incense created by using perfume and cologne sample inserts torn from magazines and ignited using the battery from my am/fm radio, other improvised tools of the arte, and an indefatigable Will, I succeeded in magickal work I am convinced would have taken me decades to master in less restrictive conditions, or in the free world, having day to day life to contend with. The loss of ones freedom is indeed a great castigation, yet in my case it became more of a gift than a curse. Having absolutely no responsibility for maintaining your own existence allows one a single minded focus in which one can devote every waking thought to furtherance of your magickal career. As a result of this, I have progressed far faster than I would have otherwise, having stood before spirits regarded as Angels, and, conversely, Demons and having learned from both, the latter more so than the former.

The translation of the *Black Dragon* was done during that period of time. It was undertaken because, despite the great lengths the chaplain went to in trying to find me a copy in English, none was to be found. One Thursday he came to my cell with the news that only a French edition could be had. This was a source of annoyance to me, since I am easily frustrated at anything being forbidden or hidden from me. I therefore ordered the French version, several versions in fact, and undertook to translate it. While working towards a translation of the *Black Dragon*, I noticed that in places its author refers to the *Enchiridion*, which subsequently led me, upon my release, since I was unable to locate even a French copy of this work while in prison, to translate the *Enchiridion* as well. The work you hold in your hand is the product of that obsessive desire to possess the unattainable.

THE WORKS

LACK DRAGON, the common name by which the French grimoire *Le Véritable Dragon Noir: Les Forces infernales soumises à l'homme* has become known, is a grimoire not at all unlike its contemporaries, in that it deals with evocation of the Infernal Forces for the purpose of forcing them to do the will of the Magus. The opening *Preface* is in fact a commentary, apparently by the Magus who set the work down on paper. In it he expounds advice and guidance which echoes that taught in nearly all of the classical grimoires, and further explains the steps of the evocations that are not found in the corpus.

The First Part, immediately following the Preface, is entitled Conjuration of the Demons and provides methodol-
ogy for evoking the four Kings, being those of the four
cardinal directions. Following this are the Conjurations to
be practiced each day of the week, along with the days and
times appropriate for summoning each of the chiefs of the
infernals and their respective seals. Interestingly enough,
while in the process of their exhaustive editorial work to
prepare *Crossed Keys* for print, Peter and Alkistis of Scarlet Imprint were able to trace the *Black Dragon*'s seals and
figures further back, tying them to those of the *Grimoire
of Honorius* as well as the *Grand Grimoire*. The latter associa-
tion furthering my own assertion that the *Black Dragon* and
the *Red Dragon*, a complete version of which has recently
been released by Teitan Press, are in fact closely related.
For this reason, and in light of the groundbreaking work
done by Jake Stratton-Kent which is leading the magickal
community to reconsider the origins and genesis of our
arte, we have decided to issue this as a corrected edition,
reproducing the illustrations as they should have been and
replacing the corrupted versions. In consideration of those
among our readers who prefer the work as it was presented in the MS from which I worked and without altera-
tion, all of the seals and figures from the Bussière edition
have been faithfully reproduced in the notes. Following
the conjurations is a collection of what, at the time this
manuscript appears to have been put to paper, we could
classify as practical applications of the magick set forth in

the tome. Examples thereof are exorcisms, incantations to protect (and to harm) animals, workings designed to prevent fatigue even when travelling long distances, creation of the sympathetic mirror, ridding a house of demons and so forth. It should be noted that while I am not one of the many who believe that in every word of a grimoire is hidden a secret, I encourage you to consider that workings which were designed for purposes such as this can be used creatively; that is to say, interpreted more fittingly for the era in which we exist. For example, the working to which is attributed the purpose of preventing the Magus from becoming weary in walking; In modern times, the equivalent of becoming weary and fatigued from long travels on foot could be jet-lag. In the operation to stop a serpent from moving against you, consider that in ancient times the serpent was a term representative of the devil, and in modern times, a deceitful or treacherous man is often given the moniker serpent or snake.

Returning to the topic at hand: *The Black Dragon*. Only once prior has this grimoire ever been put into English, that being an edition produced by Robert Blanchard and the International Guild of Occult Sciences. That edition, should you desire a copy, is available very, very rarely on the secondhand market, changing hands for sums never less than $300. This, I swear, is a testament to the tendency of occultists to assign value to books based on rarity rather than quality, since that translation is absolutely, unequivocally horrible. This, if you are familiar with IGOS, will not surprise you. Nonetheless, flawed as it was, that edition was the only English version of *The Black Dragon*, until now.

Little is certain about the origins of *Le Véritable Dragon Noir*. Although it has been widely known in grimoire circles, and is mentioned in many scholarly works on Medieval and Renaissance magick, it has been largely overlooked. Even the French original is rather obscure, with the best description I've been able to find being *Grimoire de sorcellerie contenant une foule de recettes pratiques réunies par un sorcier: charmes et contre-charmes, secrets merveilleux, la Main de gloire, la Poule noire.* (Grimoire of witchcraft, containing a collection of formulas gathered by a sorcerer: charms and counter-charms, marvelous secrets, the Hand of Glory, and the Black Hen). This edition is largely derived from the Bussière edition, pseudepigraphically ascribed to Honorius in the 15th century.

THE ENCHIRIDION OF POPE LEO III

 F THE ENCHIRIDION, in stark con-
trast to the *Black Dragon*, much is
known. We have, on this work,
not only historical provenance of
the MS, but also magickal lore and
legend attributing it to Charlemagne. While the *Enchiridion* is not
a grimoire in style of the former, it
is indeed a book outlining magickal practices and the use
of the biblical psalms for material and worldly gains.

With regard to the legend and history of the *Enchiridion*,
I defer here to A.E. Waite:

*The legend of the Enchiridion is as follows. When Charlemagne
was leaving Rome after his coronation by Leo III., that pontiff presented him with a memorial of the visit in the shape of a collection
of prayers, to which wonderful virtues were attributed. Whosoever
bore the little work upon his person with the respect due to Holy
Scripture, who also recited it daily to the honour of God, would
never be overcome by his enemies, would pass unscathed through
all perils, and the Divine protection would abide with him to the end
of his days. These things took place in the year 800. In the year 1523
the Enchiridion is supposed to have been printed at Rome for the
first time. Thus broadly outlined, there is nothing in this legend to
offend possibility or to raise very serious objection to the authorship.
The reputed connection with occult science would indeed seem the*

chief presumption against it, because there never was a literature so
founded in forgery as that of Magic, except the sister science of physical Alchemy. When we come, however, to examine the work at first
hand, the case against it assumes a different aspect, and it is condemned out of its own mouth. While it is not a Ritual of Magic, it is
also certainly not a simple collection of devotions designed to fortify
the person making use of them against dangers of body and soul
by the operation of Divine Grace; it is rather a collection of charms
cast in the form of prayers, and is quite opposed in its spirit to the
devotional spirit of the Church; furthermore, it is concerned with
worldly advantages far more than with those of a spiritual kind. The
work opens with a characteristic stultification in respect of its own
claim, by pointing out that of all the sovereign princes of past ages
there was none more fortunate than Charlemagne, and the source
of his great prosperity is acknowledged by him in a letter of thanks
addressed to Pope Leo, the original of which, it is affirmed, may still
be seen in the Library of the Vatican, written with the monarch's
own hand. He states therein that since his reception of a little volume entitled Enchiridion, filled with special prayers and mysterious
figures, sent by His Holiness as a precious gift, he has never ceased to
be fortunate, and that of all things in the universe which are capable
of harming man, not one has shewn any malignity against him, in
gratitude for which he proposes to devote himself and all that is his
to the service of his benefactor. The letter is in Latin; the monarch
styles himself Carolus Magnus, which appears highly unlikely, and
he terms the pontiff Summus Antistitum Antistes, but this is not in
itself improbable, as the Papal claim to Episcopal supremacy was
fully developed at the beginning of the ninth century.

It is needless to say that there is no such document preserved in the Vatican Library; furthermore, there are no letters of Charlemagne extant, and, despite the encouragement he gave to men of learning and the Academy mentioned by Alcuin, it is not at all certain that he could either read or write. Lastly, while it is quite true that his empire included Germany, as it did also Holland, Belgium, Switzerland and part of Italy, after his coronation it is much more probable that he would have styled himself Emperor of the Romans. There is, in fact, no colourable pretence of genuineness about the so-called autograph letter, or to be precise it betrays itself – as I have indeed suggested already. This fact being established, we may proceed to the consideration of the alleged date of publication – Rome, 1523. This edition is mentioned by Pierre Christian in his Histoire de la Magie, and he defends the authenticity of the Enchiridion on the ground, among others, that it passed unchallenged in the Eternal City during such a pontificate as that of Clement VII. A second edition is said to have been printed at Rome in 1606; between 1584 and 1633 it appeared four times at Lyons and once at Mayence. In 1660 it was published for the last time at Rome. Unfortunately for the purposes of this criticism, the examples of 1633 and 1660 have been alone available. The first claims to be nuperrime mendis omnibus purgatum, but it has been evidently in the hands of a Grimoire maker, and it appears to have been edited and extended in the Grimoire interest. This is certain, but it is impossible to say how much beyond the Seven Mysterious Orisons connected with the name of Pope Leo are to be found in the original, or whether the original was antedated. Outside these Orisons the modern accent of the work is unmistakable, and it is difficult to understand how any instructed person, much less a bibliophile like M. Christian, could have been deceived by it. It is certain, however, that when he approached the secret sciences, their substitutes and their memorials in literature, he depended more on his imagination than on his knowledge or research. The work itself, as already said, is simply a collection of religious charms, effectual against all the perils to which every sort and condition of men may be made subject on land, on water, from open and secret enemies, from the bites of wild and rabid beasts, from poisons, from fire, from tempests. While it thus ensures against evil, it gives happiness in domestic matters and in the enterprises which contribute to prosperity and to the pleasures of a contented life. The proviso is that "the instructions must be followed as accurately as human weakness will allow."

Fortunately they are more simple than the grimoires. When a copy of the book has been secured, it must be placed in a small bag of new leather, so that it may be kept clean. A vow must be made to carry it as far as practicable on one's person, and to read with attentive devotion at least one page daily. If a specific danger be apprehended, a page suitable to its nature should be selected. Reading must be done upon the knees, with the face turned to the east: "so did Charlemagne invariably." Furthermore, works of piety must be performed in honour of the celestial genii whose benign influence it is desired to attract; alms also must be given to the poor, "as this is of all things most pleasing unto such spirits, for thereby we become their coadjutors and friends, the economy of the universe being committed to them by the Creator."

Psalm magic can be found in Judaism, and became one of the staples of Cunning Craft. It continues to be utilised in Hoodoo, Vodou, by folk practitioners and in other lineages of magical Catholicism. We can even consider the Qabalistic Cross of the Golden Dawn as a form of psalm magic. Furthermore, many of the Psalms have their origins in Babylonian and Egyptian hymns and prayers of demonstrable magical intent. We also find psalm fragments embedded in the Greek Magical Papyri. Indeed, we find spells in the *Enchiridion* which are similar or identical to those in the *Black Dragon*, suggesting a continuity of European spellcraft expediently taking on, or discarding, a Christian guise.

Though it may appear alien to the modern mage, whose inclinations may favour the demonic, the owner of *Le Véritable Dragon Noir* would have no qualms following its instruction to use the Orisons from the *Enchiridion*. This is not dissimilar to the practice of dual observance in Traditional Craft.

With imagination and understanding the principles are still valid in application and these Keys are thus combined, crossed as indeed they are in the great Papal Seal.

Having now introduced both myself and the texts that I have endeavored to make available, I invite you to proceed to the corpus of this work.

THE BLACK DRAGON

The Infernal Forces
Subject to Man

Evocations
Spells & Counter-Spells
Marvelous Secrets
The Hand of Glory
The Black Hen

CONJURATION
OF THE BOOK

 CONJURE YOU, book, to be useful and beneficial to all those who read you for success in their affairs. I conjure you anew, by the blood of Jesus Christ contained in the chalice forever, to be useful to all those who read you. I exorcise you in the name of the Most Holy Trinity, in the name of the Most Holy Trinity, in the name of the Most Holy Trinity.

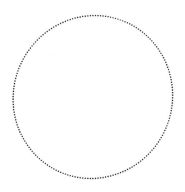

Mark of the Spirit

This book is the science of good and of evil. Whoever you may be reader, young or old, rich or poor, content or not, if your heart is tormented by Avarice, throw this book into the fire, otherwise it will be the source of all harm for you, the cause of your ruin and total doom. If, on the contrary, you possess Faith, Hope and Charity, save this book as the most precious treasure in the universe.

Thus you are warned. You are free in your actions, but do not forget that a severe account will be exacted from you for the use you will have made of the treasures I place at your disposal. As for me, a servant of God, I disclaim all responsibility, having only written this book for the good of Humanity.

PREFACE

UMBLE READER, allow me to take your hand and make with you the first steps along the arduous path which is opened for you in this work. Heed well my counsel and take advantage of it. Indeed, it is no trivial matter to have direct relations with the demons, for they are our greatest enemies, yours, mine and of all humanity, and each time they are able to bring us misfortune, there is relief and joy for them.

They will reveal themselves according to your character — that is to say, in accord with your weakness, whether you are submissive, thoughtful, polite and courteous, or loud, ostentatious, quick-tempered and threatening — with the intention of deceiving or intimidating you always for your loss and for their relief. Be composed, resolute and upright and it will be easy to avoid their traps.

4

At their appearance before the Circle, begin by enjoining them to restrain all of the abnormalities they have created; cold, heat, noise, evil odor, &c., and that obtained, make them give their solemn oath not to begin again in the future. Accept nothing from them hand to hand, and demand that all material things that you will receive from them shall be cast, without breakage or damage, into that part of the Circle which you shall have indicated to them. Never forget that the Circle is your refuge: within it you are master and king, yet outside of it you will be at the command of the evil spirit.

Sometimes, in conducting philosophical [magical] operations, you will be able to perceive something abnormal in the air that you breathe or under the roof where you live, but do not be troubled by it: it is the spirit stirring in anger at his powerlessness to prevent the realization of your plans; he knows your most secret thoughts, but he can do nothing against you.

The circles or pentacles must be made with blessed chalk or blessed charcoal. Blessed chalk means the chalk which has been left on or under the altar cloth during the Mass, or if no better can be done, simply on the blessed stone [the altar]; and, for the blessed charcoal, the charcoal taken from the boxwood of the blessed cross [the tree from which the cross of Christ was said to have been made, or dogwood, &c; also used to make coffins]. For the latter do as follows: go to the cemetery and there take of the boxwood that henceforth you will carry with you to safeguard

5

ît, for ît will serve you upon more than one occasion. One morning, during which a mass has been said at the church in your parish, light in your abode a small fire of dry and virgin wood, that is to say from bîts of wood which have not been taken from an object that has served for some profane use, and put therein the pieces of boxwood destined to be changed into charcoal. You may use tongs made of new wood to retrieve the burnt boxwood, and any new box can be used to smother the coals.

Before beginning any philosophical operation, take good care to purify your hands and body. Make your Circle according to all of the rules of the art, wîth a diameter of at least twelve feet and in such a way that there is no open space or gap in ît, as such a breach would be a doorway for the evil spirît.

Always take holy water and a blessed branch into the Circle wîth you, so that the demon can do you no harm; although to ensure you are obeyed in everything without trickery or deception, arm yourself with the mysterious stang, which you obtain in the following manner: first buy, wîthout haggling, a knife whose blade is of pure steel, and on the day that you deem the most suîtable, find yourself in the woods before sunrise. At the moment when the sun pierces the horizon, cut a rod of wild hazel of some three feet or so to serve as a handle, then go to an iron-worker who will make for you a small, erect fork with two tines from the blade of your knife: do not trust this task to anyone who will not perform the work in front of you, or else do ît yourself. When you ſpeak wîth and direct a demon, hold this book in the left hand, and your stang in the right; this ſhould be in a horizontal poſîtion, the tines turned toward the ſpirît.¹ A table can serve as a depoſîtory for all of the aforesaid objects, but they must always be wîthin hand's reach. Throughout the duration of the operation, keep a paschal candle alight, or burn ſpirît of brandy in a lamp intended solely for that purpose: consequently, you will find your powers increased ten-fold, putting, in the event of any disobedience from the ſpirît, the tines of the stang into the flame, but never make gratuîtous use of this means.

Several persons may assemble in the Circle, but only one, the Karcist, ſhould ſpeak wîth the ſpirît; the others must keep silent, even when the demon seeks to interrogate or threaten them.

The present discourse complements all that is said later on the same subject, thus take care to construe well my thought: I tell you that everything wrîtten in this book must be followed to the letter, whilst taking advantage of my counsel according to the circumstances. Thus the Demon will always demand of you a pledge [in exchange for his services], and you cannot refuse him; you ſhould not even allow him to depart wîthout gîving him a pledge. Never agree to gîve him an object derîved from your body, such as your hair, blood, &c; you ſhould understand that you cannot throw him your handkerchief eîther, since a used handkerchief contains substances drawn from your body. It is the same for certain other objects which he may request of you. Besides the pledge stipulated in the conjurations hereafter, the proper thing to do is to reach into your pocket and throw him a small coin or the first that comes to hand. When nothing to the contrary is stipulated, the pledge must be made immediately before the reading of the dismissal. For those philosophical operations which require a great number of sessions, prepare yourself, [ie. agree upon a suitable payment for the demon] but only acquiesce to any pact that is incapable of causing you harm, be it presently or in the future: you have the means to make them comply with you, use them!

If the Demon were to disappear without your consent, that is to say without having read the license to depart, put your mysterious stang into the flame, or otherwise reiterate the conjuration, and as soon as he reappears reproach him harshly for his disobedience, then continue your work. By no means leave the Circle without having read the *Conjuration and Dismissal of the Spirits*: you will find prayers at the end of this volume, I urge you to read some of them before stepping out of the Circle.

The Spirit will never come to you without being called from the heart at the same time as by the mouth, and proves once more that you must be resolute and unwavering in your Will. If you are performing the operation to obtain a sign [a seal or sigil], once the spirits in your presence enjoin their chief to make it known, throw the spirit a small round of virgin parchment, adjuring him to put on

ît his sign, that is to say his mark. Then he will return ît
to you, and you will paste ît to the first page of this book.
That done, that is to say approved and accepted, all dif-
ficulties are overcome, for you or those who read ît, in the
operations to follow.

You can read this book from beginning to end, wíthout
danger to you, at the permítted hours; you should even do
so often in order to be well versed in even the least of the
details of every operation that you may have to carry out.

The second part of this work popularizes the praxis of
a man who for half a century was the support of the good
and the terror of the wicked. Allow me, dear reader, to tell
you the name of this benefactor of humaníty: his name
is FRANÇOIS COLLET.[2] Many have blessed this name, and
I gíve you his example; may you, like him, be worthy of
your fellow human beings.

In respect of the secrets of the third part, use them; do
not abuse them!

I thought I should let you know of the Hand of Glory
and the Black Hen, but I will tell you nothing here on that
subject, since you alone must discover what you must do.
Recall only that avarice is always punished and virtue re-
warded, and that any pact signed in your blood places you
forever at the command of Satan.

Dear Reader, take advantage of the treasures I have gathered for you in this work; be happy, and walk upon the
earth doing good.

Adieu.

EVOCATIONS

CONJURATIONS OF THE DEMONS

N THE NAME of the Father, the Son and the Holy Spirit: take heed, come all Spirits. By the virtue and the power of your King, and by the seven crowns and chains of your Kings, all Spirits of Hell are compelled to appear to me before this Pentacle or Circle of Solomon, when I call them. Come all, at my behest, to do all that is within your power, being so charged! Come then, from the East, the South, the West and the North. I command you, by the virtue and power of He who is three, equal and eternal, God, invisible and consubstantial, in a word, and who has created the Heavens, the Sea, and all that which is under the Heavens.

One must say the following, before the signing of the book.

I conjure and compel you, Spirits, all and as many as you may be, to receive this book in good faith, so that every time we read the said book, or that it is read, being acknowledged both in form and merit, you appear in a fine human figure when you are called, as the reader deems it. In all circumstances, you shall make no assault on the body, soul or spirit of the reader, nor cause any harm to those who accompany him, whether by murmurings, tempests, noise, thunder, scandals, nor by injuries, privations or the execution of the commandments of said book. I conjure you to come as soon as the Conjuration is done, in order to execute, without delay, all that which is written and referred to in its place, in said book: you will obey, serve, instruct, give, and do everything within your power, for use by all who conjure you, all without deception. If, by chance, one of the Spirits summoned cannot come or appear when it would be required, he will be bound to send others bearing his power who will solemnly vow to carry out all that the reader may ask, whilst conjuring you all by the most holy names of the Almighty, living God, Elohim, Jah, El, Eloy, Tetragrammaton, to do all that is said herein. If you do not obey, or if any of you do not accept this book with a complete resignation to the will of the reader I shall constrain you to undergo a thousand years of punishments.

Afterwards, you command [the spirit] to stamp the seal, and once that is done, throw a pledge object and read the following Conjuration:

CONJURATION & DISMISSAL OF THE SPIRITS

Show the Pentacle[3] and say:

Here is the sentence which forbids you to be rebellious to our wills, and which orders you to return to your dwelling places. May peace be between You and Us, and be ready to return each time that I call you, to do my will.

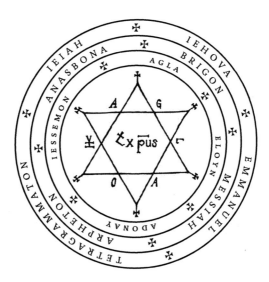

CONJURATION OF THE FOUR KINGS

These four Conjurations can be said to yourself every day and at all hours, and the Operator will use the Great Pentacle or Circle of Solomon. If one desires to speak with one Spirit only, that Spirit alone is called.

CONJURATION OF THE KING OF THE EAST

 conjure and invoke you, O powerful Magoa, King of the East, in my holy work by all the names of the Divinity, in the name of the Almighty I do command you to obey in that which you have to, to come or send N presently and without abeyance, Masseyel, Asiel, Satiel, Arduel, Acorib, and without any delay, to respond to all that I wish to know, and to do what I will command, or indeed you will come yourself to satisfy my will: and if you do not do it, I shall constrain you by all the virtue and power of God.

CONJURATION OF THE KING OF THE SOUTH

 Egym, great King of the South, I conjure and invoke you by the most high and holy names of God, to act, clothed in all your power, to come before this Circle or send me presently Fadal, Nastrachel,[4] to respond to my questions and carry out all my wishes. If you do not do it I shall compel you by God Himself.

CONJURATION OF THE KING OF THE WEST

King Bayemon! Most strong, who rules over the Western parts, I call and invoke you in the name of the Divinity. I command you, by the virtue of the Most-High to send me presently before this circle, the named one Passiel Rosusr,⁵ with all the other Spirits who are subject to you, to respond to all that I shall demand of them. If you do not do it, I shall torment you with the sword of divine fire; I shall increase your pains and I shall burn you!

CONJURATION OF THE KING OF THE NORTH

thou, Amaymon! King-Emperor of the Northern parts, I summon, invoke, exorcise and conjure you, by the virtue and power of the Creator, and by virtue of virtues, to send me presently and without delay, Madael, Laaval, Bamulbac, Belem, Ramat, with all the other Spirits who submit to you, in a fine human form: wherever you may be, come to give the honor that you owe to the living God, your Creator. In the name of the Father, the Son and the Holy Spirit, come then and be compliant before this circle and with no danger to my body or my soul, come in fine human form and not terrible, and I adjure you to come presently and at once, by all the divine names, you Sechiel, Barachiel, if you do not come swiftly, Balandier, suspensus iracundus, Origratiumgu Partus, Olemdemis et Bantatis, N. I exorcise you, invoke and do command you most highly, by the omnipotence of the true living God, by the *virtue of the holy God, and by the virtue of He who spoke and all was made, and by whose holy commandment all things have been made, Heaven, the earth and that which is in them. I adjure you by the Father, the Son and the Holy Spirit, and by the Holy Trinity, and by God whom you cannot resist, under whose empire I shall compel you to yield; I conjure you by God the Father, by God the Son, by the Holy Spirit and by the Mother of Jesus Christ, holy mother and perpetual virgin, and by Her sacred womb and by Her blessed milk which the Son of the Father sucked, and by her most sacred body and soul, and by all the parts and members of this Virgin, and by all the sorrows, afflictions, labors and bitterness which she suffered during the course of her life, by all the sobs and holy tears she shed as her dear Son wept in the time of his painful passion, upon the tree of the Cross; by all the holy sacred things which are offered and done, and others, in Heaven as on Earth, in honor of Our Lord Jesus Christ and the Blessed Mary, His mother, and by whatsoever is heavenly, by the militant Church, in honor of the Virgin and all the saints, and by the Holy Trinity, and by all other mysteries, and by the sign of the Cross, and by the most precious blood and water which flowed from the side of Jesus Christ, and by his Annunciation, and by sweat which issued from his whole body, when in the Garden of Olives he said: My father, if it is your Will that these things pass from me, that I not drink of the chalice of the dead; by his death and passion, and by his sepulchre, and by his glorious resurrection, by his ascension, by the coming of the Holy Spirit. I adjure you, once more, by the crown of thorns which he bore upon his head, by the blood which flowed from his feet and his hands, by the nails with which he was hung from the tree of the Cross, and by the five wounds, by the sa-*

cred tears which he shed, and by all that which he willingly suffered
for love of us. By the lungs, by the liver and the entrails, and by all
the limbs of Our Lord Jesus Christ; by the judgment of the living and
the dead, by the gospel of Our Lord Jesus Christ; by his preaching,
by his words, by all his miracles, by the infant in swaddling clothes,
by the crying child borne by the mother in her most precious and
virginal womb; by the glorious intercessions of the Virgin, mother
of Our Lord Jesus Christ; by all that which is of God and of his most
sacred Mother, in Heaven as on the Earth; by the holy Angels and
Archangels, and all the blessed orders of the Spirits; by the holy patriarchs and prophets, and by all the holy martyrs and confessors,
and by all the holy virgins and innocent widows, and by all the
Saints and the name of God. I conjure you by the head of Saint John
the Baptist, by the milk of Saint Catherine and by all the Blessed.

CONJURATION

A very powerful conjuration which can be said every day
and at any hour of the day or night to gain possession of
hidden treasures – whether concealed by men or by spirits
– or have them brought to you.

 command you, Demons who reside in these places,
or wheresoever in the world you may be, and whatever power which you have been given by God and
the holy Angels over this same place, and from the
powerful principality of the abyss of Hell, and all of
your confederates, both general and special, Demons of whatever or-

der you may be, whether living in the East, West, South and North, and in all directions of the Earth, by the power of God the Father, by the wisdom of God the Son, by the virtue of the Holy Spirit, and by the authority which has been given me by Our Lord Jesus Christ, the only son of the Almighty Creator, who has created us and all creatures from nothing, who caused you to have no power to hold, dwell or remain in that place, by whom I compel and command you, may you, without any falseness nor deceit, reveal to me your names, and may you leave me the peaceful power of this place; and from whatever legion you may be, and wheresoever in the world you live, on behalf of the Most Holy Trinity and by the merits of the most Blessed Virgin, and all the Saints, I unleash you all, Spirits who dwell in this place, and send you forth to the deepest depths of the Infernal Abyss. Thus, go all you cursed, damned Spirits, to the eternal fire which is prepared for you and for all your companions, if you are rebellious and defiant with me; I conjure you by the same authority, I exhort and summon you, I constrain and command you, by all the powers of your superior demons to come obey and respond favourably to what I shall command you to in the name of Jesus Christ, by whom if you or they do not promptly and without delay obey, I shall increase in short your torment in hell for a thousand years; I constrain you thus to appear here in fine human form, by the most holy names of God: Hain, Lon, Hilan, Sabaoth, Helim, Radiaha, Ledieha, Adonay, Jehova, Ya, Tetragrammaton, Sadai, Massias, Agios, Ischiros, Emmanuel, Agla, Jesus who is Alpha and Omega, the beginning and the end, may you be justly established in the fire, so that once more you will have no power to inhabit, dwell, or remain in this place, and I demand that you so do by virtue of the aforesaid names, and may the archangel Saint Michael send you to the deepest pit of Hell, in the name of the Father, the Son and the Holy Spirit, so be it.

I conjure you, Acham, or whosoever you may be, by the most holy Names of God, by Malhame, Jac, May, Mabron, Jacob, Desmedias, Eloy, Aterestin, Janastardy, Finis, Agios, Ischyros, Otheos, Athanatos, Agla, Jehova, Homosion, Aja, Messier, Sother. Christus vincit, Christus regnat, Christus imperat. Increatur Spiritus sanctus.

I conjure you, Cassiel, or whosoever you may be, by all the aforesaid names, with force I exorcise you. I advise you again by the other aforesaid names of the most great Creator which are imparted to you and shall be again hereafter, so that you heed my words, immediately and from now on, and that you observe them as inviolably as the sentences of the last day of Judgment, at which you must obey me faithfully; and do not think of rebuffing me because I am a sinner, but know that you rebuff the commandments of the most high God. Do you not know that you waste your strength before your creator and ours? Therefore think of what you reject; especially as I am promising and swearing by the last day of Judgment, and by He who created All with a single word, and whom all creatures obey. P. per sedem Baldarcy et per gratiam et diligentem tuam habuisti ab eo hanc nalatima namilam, so I ask you.

CONJURATIONS FOR
EACH DAY OF THE WEEK

MONDAY
Conjuration for Lucifer

 conjure you, Lucifer, by the living God, by the true *God, by the holy God, by the God who spoke and all was made; he commanded and all things were brought into being and created. I conjure you by the ineffable name of God On, Alpha and Omega,* Eloy, Elohim, Yah, Saday, Lux, les Mugiens, Rex, Salus, Adonay, Emmanuel, Messias, and I adjure, conjure and exorcise you by the names which are declared by the letters V, C, X; and by the names Jebova, Sol, Agla, Riffasoris, Oriston, Orphitue, Phaton Ipreto, Ogia, Speraton, Imagon, Amul, Penaton, Soter, Tetragrammaton, Eloy, Premoton, Sirmon, Perigaron, Irataton, Plegaton, On, Perchiram, Tiros, Rubiphaton, Simulaton, Perpi, Klarimum, Tremendum, Meray, and by the highest ineffable names of God, Gali, Euga, El, Habdanum, Ingadum, Obu, Euglabis, may you come to me or send N in fine and human form without any ugliness, to respond in real truth to all I shall ask him, having neither the power to injure my body nor my soul, nor whomever it may be.

This operation is to be done from 11 o'clock until 12, and from 3 o'clock until 4. It is necessary to make the circle[6] with charcoal of the blessed cross, around which the following is written: *I forbid you Lucifer, in the name of the most Holy Trinity, to enter this circle.*

The pledge which is agreeable to him is a live mouse. The master must have a stole and holy water, with an alb and surplice[7] in order to begin the conjuration without a care, to command ardently and strongly, as a master to a servant, with all kinds of threats: *Satan, Rantam, Pallantre, Lutais, Cricacœur, Scircigneur, I entreat you most humbly to give me...* [command]

Figure 2

TUESDAY
Conjuration for Frimost

 conjure you Frimost, and command you by all the names by which you may be constrained and bound, I exorcise you Nambrosth, by your name, by the virtue of all the Spirits, by all the characters, by the Pentacle of Solomon, by the Judaic, Greek and Chaldean conjurations, by your confusion and malediction, and I will intensify your pains and torments from day to day for evermore, if you do not come now to accomplish my will, and be submissive to all that I shall command of you, without having the power to harm me, or those in my company, either in body or soul.

This operation is done at night, from 9 o'clock until 10. One must give him the first stone[8] found during the day. It is in order to be received in dignity and honor. From here proceed as for Monday, and make a circle[9] around which is written: *Obey me Frimost, obey me Frimost, obey me Frimost.*

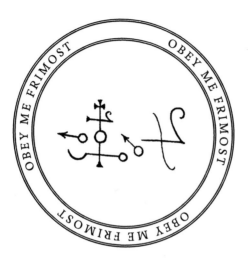

Figure 3

WEDNESDAY
Conjuration for Astaroth

 conjure you, Astaroth, wicked spirit, by the words and virtues of God, and by the powerful God, Jesus Christ of Nazareth to whom all demons are subject, who was conceived by the Virgin Mary, by the mystery of the angel Gabriel; I conjure you once more in the name of the Father and of the Son, and of the Holy Spirit, in the name of the glorious Virgin Mary and of the Most Holy Trinity, in honour of which all the archangels, the thrones, the dominations, the powers, the patriarchs, the prophets, the Apostles, and the Evangelists singing without end Holy, Holy, Holy, the Lord of Hosts, who is, who was, who will come as a river of burning fire, may you not neglect my orders, and may you not refuse to come. I command you by He who will come in flames to judge the living and the dead, to whom is due all honour, praise and glory. Come swiftly then, obey my will, come then to give praise to the true God, to the living God, and to all his works, and do not neglect to obey me and to honour the Holy Spirit: it is in his name that I command you.

This operation is done at night from 10 o'clock until 11; it is in order to have the good graces of the king and others. In the circle [10] the following is written: *Come Astaroth, come Astaroth, come Astaroth.*

Figure 4

THURSDAY
Conjuration for Silcharde

 conjure you Silcharde, *by the image and likeness of Jesus Christ our Lord, who by His death and passion redeemed the human race, who wills that, by His providence, you are present here at once. I command you by all the kingdoms of God. Act, I adjure you and compel you by His holy name, by He who trod on the serpent, who crushed the lion and the dragon, may you have to obey me and fulfil my commands, without having the power to harm me, or anyone else, either in body or in soul.*

This operation is done at night, from 3 o'clock until 4, during which time he is called and appears in the form of a king. It is necessary to give him a piece of bread so that he departs: he renders a man happy and also discovers Treasures. Around this circle[11] write the following: *By the holy God, by the holy God, by the holy God.*

Figure 5

FRIDAY
Conjuration for Bechard

 conjure you Bechard and compel you to come
to me; I conjure you once more by the most
holy name of God, Eloy, Adonay, Eloy, Agla,
Samalabaðany,[12] which are written in Hebrew,
Greek and Latin; by all the sacraments, all the
names written in this book, and by He who expelled you from the
heights of heaven. I conjure and command you, by the virtue of the
most holy Euðarist which has redeemed men from their sins, may
you come without delay to execute and fulfil all my commands,
without any wound to my body or my soul, neither doing harm to
my book, nor against those who are here with me.

This operation is to be done at night, from 11 o'clock until
12; he must be given a walnut. In his circle is written:[13]
Come Bechard, come Bechard, come Bechard.

Figure 6

SATURDAY
Conjuration for Guland

conjure you Guland, in the name of Satan, in the name of Beelzebuth, in the name of Astaroth, and in the name of all other spirits, to come unto me; come, then, to me, in the name of Satan and of all the other demons; come to me, then, when I command you to in the name of the most holy Trinity; come without doing me any harm, without wounding either my body or soul, without doing damage to my books or anything which I make use of. I command you to come without delay or send me another spirit who has the same power as you, who will accomplish all my commands and is submissive to my will, without which he whom you send, if you do not come yourself, cannot leave without my consent nor without having fulfilled my will.

This operation is done at night from 11 o'clock until 12, and as soon as he appears, he must be given some charred bread, then ask of him whatever you will; he will obey you at once. Write in his circle:[14] *Do not enter Guland, do not enter Guland, do not enter Guland.*

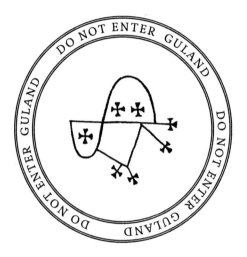

Figure 7

SUNDAY

Conjuration for Surgat

 conjure you Surgat, by all the names written in this book, may you come here now, promptly and without delay, prepared to obey me, or otherwise send me a spirit who will bring me a stone which will render me invisible to anybody whatsoever when I carry it; and I conjure you to find yourself submissive to him or those whom you send to me, to carry out and accomplish my will and all that I shall command, doing injury neither to me, nor anyone else, with the full understanding of what I want.

This operation is done at night from 11 o'clock until 1. He will ask for a hair from your head, but instead give him one from a fox, and compel him to accept it.[15] Write in his circle:[16] *Tetragrammaton* (3 times), *Ismael, Adonay, Ilma*; and in a second circle: *Come Surgat, come Surgat, come Surgat!*

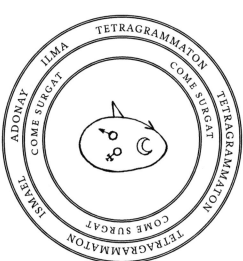

Figure 8

THE GREAT EXORCISM

TO DISPOSSESS THE HUMAN CREATURE
OR SENSELESS ANIMALS

 EMON, come out of the body of N by the commandment of God whom I adore, and give way for the Holy Spirit. I put the sign of the holy cross of Our Lord Jesus Christ on your brow, in the name of the Father and of the Son, and of the Holy Spirit. I make the sign of the cross of Our Lord Jesus Christ upon your chest, in the name of the Father, and of the Son, and of the Holy Spirit. Eternal and almighty God, Father of Our Lord Jesus Christ, cast your eyes with mercy upon your servant N whom you have deigned to call to the right faith, cure his heart of all kinds of elements and misfortunes, and break all of his chains and bonds; open, Lord, the door to your glory by your benefaction, that being marked by the seal of your wisdom, he will be free of the stench, the attacks and the desires of the unclean spirit; and being filled with the sweet smell of your goodness and grace, he will observe the commandments of your Church with joy; and advancing day by day towards perfection, he is made worthy of having received the salutary remedy to his faults, by your holy baptism, by the merits of Jesus Christ Our Lord, and God: Lord, we beg you to hear our prayers, to save

34

us and protect that which a merciful love made you redeem at the price of your precious blood, and by the virtue of your holy cross, with which we are marked. Jesus, protector of the afflicted poor, be propitious to the people whom you have adopted, we who are participants in the new testament, so that the letters of the promise be fulfilled, to have received by your grace that which they could only hope for through you Jesus Christ Our Lord, our recourse, who has made the heaven and the earth. I exorcise you, creature, in the name of God the almighty Father, and by the love which Our Lord Jesus Christ bore, and by the virtue of the Holy Spirit. I exorcise you by the great living God who is the true God whom I adore, and by the God who created you, who has preserved all His elect, who commanded his servants to bless them, for the use of those who believe in him, so that everything becomes a beneficial sacrament to drive out the enemy. It is for this, Lord our God, that we beseech you to bless this salt by your holy benediction, and to make of it a perfect remedy unto those who shall receive it; may it abide in their entrails, so that they are incorruptible in the name of Our Lord Jesus Christ who shall judge the living and the dead, and by the seal of the God of Abraham, of the God of Isaac, of the God of Jacob, of the God who showed himself to his servant Moses on Mount Sinai, who took the children of Israel out of Egypt, giving them an angel to divide and to lead them day and night. I beg you, Lord, to send your holy angel to protect your servant N and to lead him to eternal life, under your holy baptism. I exorcise you, impure and rebellious spirit, in the name of the Father, God the Son, and God the Holy Spirit; I command you to leave the body of N, I adjure you to retire in the name of He who offered His hand to Saint Peter when he was close

35

to drowning in the water. Obey your God, evil demon, and the sentence which is pronounced against you, and honour the living God, honor the Holy Spirit and Jesus Christ the only Son of the Father. Withdraw, ancient serpent, from the body of N as the great God commands you to; may your pride be utterly confounded and annihilated before the sign of the holy cross, by which we are marked by the baptism and grace of Jesus Christ. Think on how the day of your ordeal approaches, and that extreme torments await you; that your judgment is irrevocable, that your sentence condemns you to the eternal flames, along with all of your companions, for your rebellion against your Creator. This is why, cursed demon, I order you to flee on behalf of the God whom I adore, flee! by the holy God, by the true God, by He who spoke and all was made; give praise to the Father, to the Son and to the Holy Spirit, and to the most holy and indivisible Trinity. I command you, sordid Spirit, whomsoever you are, to come out of the body of this creature N, created by God, the same God who is Jesus Christ Our Lord; may He stoop today, in his infinite kindness, to call you in grace to share in His holy sacraments which he has instituted for the salvation of all the faithful; in the name of God who will judge the whole world by fire.

Here is the Cross of Our Lord Jesus Christ ✠ [make the sign of the Cross]. Flee! Enemies be gone: here is the Lion of the tribe of Judah, Root of David.

SPELLS & COUNTER-SPELLS

FOR LIFTING ANY SPELL
& SUMMONING THE PERSON WHO HAS CAUSED HARM

Take the heart of a dead animal taking care not to make a single wound to ît, and put ît upon a clean plate; then get nine thorns from a hawthorn and proceed as follows:

Pierce the heart wîth one of the thorns saying: *Adibaga, Saboath, Adonay, contra ratout prisons pererunt fini unixio paracle gossum.*

Take two of your thorns and press them in saying: *Qui fussum mediator agros gaviol valax.*

Take two others and piercing ît say: *Landa zazar valoi sator salu xio paracle gossum.*

Take two of your other thorns and whilst piercing pronounce: *Mortus cum fice sunt et per flagellationem Domini Nostri Jesu-Christi.*

Finally, pierce ît wîth the last two thorns, saying the following words: *Avir sunt paracletur stator verbonum offisum fidando.*

Then continue saying: *I call those who made the Good Missal; cowardly have you done evil, come to us from everywhere you are found, by the sea or by the earth, everywhere, wîthout delay and wîthout forfeît.*

Pierce the heart with a thorn with these last words. Note
that if one is unable to obtain thorns of hawthorn, one
may have recourse to new nails instead. The heart, being
pierced as we have indicated, is placed in a small bag then
hung in the chimney,[17] high enough that it cannot be seen.
The next day retrieve the heart from the bag and place it
on a plate. Extracting the first thorn, pierce it into another
point in the heart while pronouncing the words that we
have specified above; draw out another two thorns and
re-pierce them saying the appropriate words; finally, draw
them all out in the same order to re-pierce them as prescribed, observing never to press them into the same holes.
This work continues for nine days. However, if you do not
want to give the malefactor any release you make a novena the same day, and in the prescribed order [of Catholic
dogma]. After having finally pierced the nail into the heart
while pronouncing the aforesaid words, one makes a large
fire; afterwards the heart is placed on a grill and roasted
on the scorching brazier. The malefactor will be compelled
to come and ask for pardon. If it is outside his power to
come in the short time that you accord him you intensify
this burning. Note well that you must prevent the evil-
doer approaching your grill by barring the door, or by all
other means.

TO DISRUPT & DESTROY ALL EVIL SPELLS
PERFORMED AGAINST ANIMALS

Take a cup of salt, more or less, according to the number of cursed animals, and pronounce before ît that whiĉh follows: *Hergo gomethunc geridans sesserant délibérant amci.*

Then make three turns around the animals, beginning on the side of the rising sun, and continuing following the course of that star,[18] wîth the animals before you, and, whilst doing so you throw some pinĉhes of salt on them, recîting the same words.

THE SYMPATHETIC MIRROR

This mirror, whiĉh has the form indicated by figure 9,[19] is double-glazed, plain on one side and magnifying on the other. These two surfaces are called reŝpeĉtîvely the small side and the large side of the mirror. The sympathetic mirror is employed in certain operations of counter-ŝpells in order to know the evil-doer: One looks into ît, sometimes on one side, sometimes on the other, pronouncing the words indicated, and, at a gîven moment, the figure of the operator disappears, and is replaced by that of the evil-doer who comes and goes more or less often.

When ît is worked so as to relieve a person in whom illness is already very advanced, ît is sometimes necessary to touch the patient with the mirror repeating the mysterious words said in the operation of counter-spells.

Figure 9

The sympathetic mirror possesses, moreover, certain natural virtues, among these those of curing the pain of deafness and rheumatic ills in general. For this one touches the part of the body corresponding to the pain, alternately with one side of the mirror and the other, without regard to which side one begins, each time devoting the ill one to the three Saints, saying for example: *Saint Joseph, Saint John, Saint Jacques, I implore you to cure N.* Repeat this three times, then say three *Our Fathers* and three *Hail Marys* whilst, before and after, making the sign of the cross. Recommend the patient to rub the place of the illness with fingers moistened wîth salîva, once a day for three days, and each time to say three *Our Fathers* and three *Hail Marys*, as above.

In order to have such a mirror one buys one glazed wîth two sides conforming to the sympathetic mirror, and, in an evocation, one conjures the spirît known to him by the virtues stipulated in this book, by whom ît cannot be refused. In the case where he will ask to touch the mirror, ît will be necessary to throw the spirît the mirror enjoining him to then place ît back into the circle wîthout cracking ît and endowing ît wîth the aforesaid virtues.

This mirror must never serve a single profane use.

OF THE TALISMAN,
ITS CONSTRUCTION & ITS VIRTUES

On the Eve of Saint John the Baptist,[20] between one o'clock and two in the morning, go to where there is wild periwinkle or dwarf perîwinkle[21] growing. It can be had from the garden, or flower pots, whilst noting in this last case that the pots must be placed in such a way that one will be obliged to leave home in order to go to them. The plant is gathered in silence and brought into the house, taking due care not to look back, even if you hear the sound of footsteps behind your heels; no evil, moreover, can befall the operator during this journey, all animals will flee at his approach. It is then saved to be used for the following purpose.

Take, so far as you can, the first stalk that your eyes fall
upon when you open the box containing the gathered
flowers above; take off the head and place ît on a small
piece of whîte paper, then complete the number of leaves
adding, from the same brandh, in order to have nine of
them; afterwards, add to ît a pea of camphor and fold. As
soon as the paper has been folded in two, and you are no
longer, by consequence, able see îts contents, say while
continuing to fold the paper:

1 If you wiśh to use this padket as a talisman: *For N(Name
the person), lîving at ... (place), whom we wiśh to save from all evil
śpells, for N*, once [folding the paper recîte these Latin words
of magic] – *vassis atatlos vesul et cremus, verge san hergo diaboliâ
herbonos*, twice – *vassis atatlos etc*, three times – *vassis*, etc.

2 If you wiśh to employ ît in order to break & destroy an
evil śpell [say]: *For N, lîving at ..., whom we wiśh to cure of an evil
śpell if he (or śhe) has one, and against one so and so* (he or śhe
who cast the evil śpell), once – (say the above Latin words
again), twice ..., three times ..., etc.

Whilst making the padket, hold the paper pressed against
the small side of the mirror; when ît is done, toudh ît to
the large [magnifÿing] side and then gîve ît to the named
person, as follows:

1 If this is to be used as a talisman, ît is taken in the right hand, the sign of the cross is made and ît is worn as a scapular wrapped in linen [hung about the neck]. Its virtue lasts a year; at the end of this time throw ît into the fire.

2 If ît is for healing, ît is taken in the right hand as well, making the sign of the cross and attaching ît to the shirt (of the ill one) in such a way that ît comes into contact with the skin, in the place of the ailment. Watch ît for three days, or five if more force is wished. At the end of that time, either the operator or the patient takes the packet, makes the sign of the cross, puts ît into the fire covering ît with coals, and leaves immediately; setting foot outside say: *God save us.*

The packet and the words serve several ends. Note that the operator can keep the packet[22] on him, place ît in his pocket, and carry ît to the cursed one.

TO TAKE CARE IN RETURNING FROM THE HOUSE OF A PERSON WHO YOU WISH TO HEAL

Proceed to a crossroads, the best is a four-way, but take the first that you come to; throw a small coin in the middle of the crossing with force saying: *Keep that, pick up your spoils,* and leave without looking back.

TO DESTROY A SPELL & SEE THE EVIL-DOERS PASS
(IN THE MIRROR)

Buy a new earthenware pot with a lid, large enough to hold five sous' worth of camphor, a bundle of needles, the heart of a bullock, (if need be one can use the heart of a female calf) – all bought without haggling.[23]

Bar the door well where the operation will be done.

Place the heart upon a clean plate and there prick it with the needles, one by one, repeating with each piercing the following words which we already know: *Against N* (if you know the person you say their name or, *he whom intends me harm*, if unknown), once – *vassis atatlos vesul et cremus, verbo san hergo diabolia herbonos;* twice – repeat the words, etc; three times – repeat, etc.

The operation completed, place the heart in the pot with the camphor and three drops of holy water; put the pot on the fire at exactly 11:30 and allow it to boil until at least one hour after midnight. The next day bury the pot in the ground in an uncultivated spot.

In order to see the evil-doer, bring the pot to a boil, from beginning to end, and every five minutes or so repeat the words given above whilst looking into the mirror, sometimes one side, sometimes the other: it is rare that one will not see the evil-doers come and go in the mirror.

Note: take good care not to leave, and that no-one in the house leaves, for the duration of the operation. It is well to give a packet to the patient before beginning the operation.

It is necessary to make a novena, that is to say during nine other days, at 11:30 evenings and mornings, one repeats the words above.

TO LIFT A SPELL OR RID A HOUSE OF DEMONS

Give a packet to the cursed one [of the house], or hang it in the chimney in a sack of new cloth [usually linen]. If the person is mad, you must have three Masses said in three different parishes, and the family in the house, at the hour of the Masses, should say together the *Credo*, making the sign of the cross, say three *Our Fathers*, and three *Hail Marys*, make anew the sign of the cross, and say the *Veni Creator*.

This done, place yourself in the South, having in your left hand holy water and in your right holy boxwood, and say: *O God of the South, O God of the East, O God of the West, O God of the North, evil spell that I should have corrupted on your lives.*

Pronounce these words three times, and each time take the holy water and strongly asperge it to the right and to the left.[24] Make a novena looking into the mirror, if one has one, with the words already cited.

TO BREAK & DESTROY A SPELL
BY THE MEANS OF THE BLACK COCK

Take a black cockerell, feed him with three drops of holy
water and hang him by the legs in a loft where you leave
him three full days. The time having passed, take him
by the legs and bury him in the warm dung of a sheep
pen, having taken care that no-one can go and remove it.
The evil one will fall ill, and die after languishing for six
months or a year.

In performing the above operations, pronounce the
words that we have already made known: *Against N, vassis atatlos vesul et cremus, verbo san hergo diabolia herbonos*, &c.
Also take good care to lock the loft while the rooster is in
it.

TO DIVERT A PERSON

Take a toad before sunrise or after sunset; feed him with a
piece of camphor with a skewer of wood or iron, or even
a nail;[25] thread his two jaws with the said skewer; tie the
jaws with a thread and hang him in the chimney high
enough that he will not be seen. In doing that which pre-
cedes, from start to finish, say: *I will that you burst, you who
has done the evil. Against you, once vassis*, &c. Make a novena.

Take a twig of wild larch wood, a twig of holly and a
third of wild hazel, each three feet long. Put them into
a fire built of dry wood and burn them starting with one

end. Once they begin to burn and until they are done, say as above, and make the novena.[26]

TO WARD OFF A BAD ENCOUNTER

Take three steps backwards looking continually at the person and say: *Against you! Verbo san diaboliâ herbonos.*

TO MAKE A PERSON SUFFER

Operate on the last Friday of the month, in the morning, on an empty stomach.

Take a piece of lard, as large as an egg; prick it with pins (about thirty, without counting them), saying the words: once, *vassis atatlos*, etc; place on top two branches of blessed bough in a cross,[27] and bury it all in non-cultivated ground.

TO IMMOBILIZE AND MAKE A PERSON SUFFER

Go to a cemetery and there pick up a nail from an old coffin, saying: *Nail, I take you that you may serve me to deter and do harm to all persons that I wish; in the name of the Father, and of the Son, and of the Holy Spirit. Amen.*

When you wish to leave, trace the figure given below on a piece of new board and drive the nail into the middle of the triangle, saying: *Pater Noster* up to *in terra*; afterwards strike upon the nail with a stone saying: *You do evil to N until I take you from there.* Cover the spot with a little powder or dust, and remember well the spot, for one cannot cure the evil that it has caused until you draw the nail out and say: *I withdraw you so that the evil that you have caused to N ceases in the name of the Father, and of the Son, and Holy Spirit. Amen.*

Then take the nail and erase the characters, not with the same hand that made them, but with the other, since otherwise it will be of danger to the curser.

Figure 10

MARVELOUS SECRETS

THE CASTLE OF BEAUTY
PROTECTION FOR HORSES & SHEEP

AKE SALT on a plate, then having your back turned to the rising Sun, and the animals in front of you, pronounce, on bended knee and with head bare, that which follows: *Salt which is made and formed at the Castle of the good beautiful Saint Elizabeth, in the name of Disolet, Soffet carrying salt, salt of salt, I conjure you, in the name of Gloria, Doriante and Galianné her sister; salt, I entreat you to help me keep my horses alive, these steeds present here before God and I, and keep them healthy and clean, well fed and watered, and large and fat, that they may be as I desire: salt of salt, I conjure you, by the power of glory and by the virtue of glory, and in my every intention always for glory.*

49

That pronounced in the direction of the rising Sun [East], take the other direction following the course of that star, and there pronounce that which follows below. You do the same at the other directional quarters, and once you have returned to the point where you began, pronounce anew the same words. Arrange it so that during the entire ceremony the animals are always in front of you, because those which cross will be as mad beasts.

Then make three turns around your horses, throwing pinches of your salt upon the animals, saying: *Salt I cast thee by the hand which God has given me; Hook, I take thee, thou I was expecting.*

In the remainder of your salt you bleed the animal on which you mount, saying: *Horse, I bleed you by the hand which God has given me; Hook, I take thee, thou I was expecting.*

One must let the blood with a piece of hard wood, such as boxwood or pear tree; the blood is drawn from such a part as you wish, taking care that the animal has its rear behind you. If it is a sheep, you take its head between your legs. After the bloodletting, you lift the horny part of the right foot, that is to say you cut a piece from the hoof on the right foot, with a knife, then you part this piece in two and make a cross with it; you put this cross in a piece of new cloth and cover it with your salt. You then take some wool if you are working with sheep, otherwise some horsehair, you also make a small cross with it that you put in your cloth on the salt; you place upon that wool or horsehair a second layer of salt. You next make another small cross out of virgin wax or a blessed candle, then you put your remaining salt over it, and tie it all in a ball with a string. With this ball, rustle the animals out of the stable, if they are horses; if sheep, rustle them out of the barn or sheepfold, pronouncing the words which are to be employed for casting the salt; continue to swish or rustle them for one, two, three, seven, nine or eleven days afterwards, according to the strength or vigor of the animals.

Note well that you should not do your throwing until the last word. When you work on horses, deliver the words strongly; in the case of sheep, the longer and milder your delivery the more effective you will be. All of the protections begin on the Tuesday or Friday of the crescent moon, that is, in its waxing phase. It is also necessary to take good care that your balls not take on moisture, for the animals will perish. The balls are usually carried in the fob-pocket, but if you do not carry them with care, do as expert practitioners do, put them near you in some dry safe place, and have no fear. We have stated here-above to take only the horny part of the right foot to use in the ball. The majority go on to take it from all four feet and consequently make two small crosses from it since they have four pieces thus obtained, but this is superfluous and produces nothing more in effect. If you do all the ceremonies of the four quarters to the direction of the rising sun, this will be well since the flock or herd will be less dispersed.

It can be remarked that an evil shepherd, who wants to replace you, is capable of causing you much distress, and

even make the flock perish: primarily by the means of the
ball which he cuts into pieces and which he spreads upon a
table or elsewhere; by the means of a mole or a weasel, or
yet again by means of a frog or a green tree-frog[28] which he
puts into an anthill, saying: *Maudition, perdition*, etc. (From
the *Enchiridon*). He leaves it there for nine days, at the end
of which he digs it up with the same words, and after having been ground into a powder, it is scattered where the
flock will graze. Use can again be made of the three nails
taken from different cemeteries and, by means of certain
words we do not wish to reveal, one can cause as many
animals as one wants to perish. We shall give at length the
manner of breaking and destroying these conjurings.

AGAINST COLIC, WOUNDS & INFECTIONS OF HORSES

Pass the hand over the side of the horse under the belly
and say: *Horse (name the coat color), belonging to N, if you have
sores, of whatever coloration that they may be of red trench disease
or infection or what may come to be sliced or irritated, or of the
thirty six kinds of other illnesses,*[29] *in the case which here may be,
God and the blessed Saint Eloy*[30] *will cure you: In the name of the
Father, and of the Son and of the Holy Spirit.* Afterwards say five
Our Fathers and five *Hail Marys*, whilst kneeling, and make
the horse swallow a handful of gray salt dissolved in a pint
of tepid water.

IN ORDER THAT LAMBS BECOME HEALTHY & STRONG

Take the first born, or failing him the first comer, and raise
him from the ground with the nose towards you, saying:
Ecce lignum crucem in quo salus mundi crucem.[31] Place him back
upon the earth, raise him again and say as above three
times. That done, you utter softly the Orison of the day
whichever it may be, which you will find in the *Enchiridion*.

TO CURE A CANCER OR OTHER ILLNESS ACCESSIBLE
TO THE EYES & FINGERS

With the master finger (the longest), make the turn of
harm thrice whilst following the course of the Sun, saying
each time: *Evil illness N, it is said that you have as many roots
here as God has friends in Heaven.* Perform this operation for
three days in a row, before sunrise. In turning the finger,
do not raise it from above the skin.

AGAINST BURNS

*Saint Lazarus and Our Lord Jesus Christ themselves went into a
holy village. Saint Lazarus said to Our Lord: I hear on high a great
cry. Our Lord said to him: It is an infant who burns, go there, and
you shall cure him of his fever.* Three times these words are
pronounced over the burns fever sores or lesions sending

each time a breath against them, then apply a compress well soaked in olive oil.

TO RECOVER STOLEN OBJECTS

Burn a good handful of street dirt and a worn out shoe, and say the *Credo* prayer thrice, making the sign of the cross before and after.

TO SEE IN A VISION AT NIGHT WHAT YOU DESIRE
TO KNOW OF THE PAST OR FUTURE

In the evening, before you go to sleep, reproduce fig. 11 on virgin parchment. The two *N*s indicate the place where you should place your names, and what you desire to know. The free space between the two circles is intended to receive the name of the angels whom you desire to invoke. This done, recite the following Orison three times and sleep on your right side with your ear on the parchment.

Orison

O glorious name of the great living God, whom through all time, and in whom all things are present, I who am your servant N... (your name), Eternal Father, I beg you to send me your angels, those who are written in the circle, that they will show me that which I am

curious to know and understand, by Jesus Christ Our Savior and
Lord. Amen.[32]

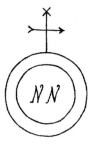

Figure 11

TO STOP A SERPENT

Throw at him a piece of paper soaked in a solution of al-
um-water and upon which you shall have written with the
blood of a kid: *Stop fair one, here is a pledge.* Afterwards you
swish at him with a willow wand:[33] If he is touched with
this wand he will die right away, or he will swiftly flee.

TO STOP HORSES & CARRIAGES

Trace upon black paper, with white ink, the pentacle rep-
resented by figure 12, and throw this pentacle at the head
of the horses saying: *White or black horse, whatever color you*
may be, it is I who makes you do this; I conjure you that you can no

longer move your feet, as you do your ears, no more than Beelze-buth can break his fetters. It is necessary, for this experiment, to have a nail forged during the midnight Mass, which you will drive into where the harness joins. Failing that, take a fastening which you conjure as follows: *I conjure you in the name of Lucifer, Beelzebuth and of Santanas, the three princes of all of the devils, that you shall have to stop yourselves.*[34] During the three days before that on which you desire to carry out this experiment, you must take care not to do any Christian work.

Figure 12

COUNTER-SPELL

Hostia sacra verra corrum, casting out the great devil of hell, all words, enchantments and characters which have here been said, read and celebrated upon the bodies of my living horses, let them

be utterly broken behind me. After that you recite the Orison
which begins with these words: *Word which was made flesh…*
(As found in the *Enchiridon*).

TO APPEAR TO BE ACCOMPANIED BY MANY

Take a handful of sand and conjure it thus: *Anachi, Jehova,
Hœlersa, Azarabel, rets caras sapor aye pora cacotamo Iopidon
ardagal margas poston eulia buget Kephar, Solzeth, Karne phaca
ghedolossalese tata.* Put the sand thus conjured in an ivory
box with the powdered skin of a tiger-snake.[35] Then, throw
it in the air whilst repeating the conjuration, and as many
men as there are grains of sand will appear, on the days
and in the hours that the Sun is in the sign of Mary the
Virgin.

TO RENDER ONESELF INVISIBLE

Steal a black cat, and without haggling, buy a new pot, a
mirror, a flint, an agate stone, and some coal & tinder, at
the stroke of midnight fetch water from a fountain, after which you should light your fire. Then put the cat in
the pot and the pot on the fire, holding the lid with the
left hand, without moving nor looking behind, no matter
if you should hear a noise; and after having boiled it for
twenty-four hours, put it on a new plate; take the meat
and throw it over the left shoulder, saying these words:

Accîpe quod tibi do, et nihil amplius. Then, place the bones one
by one between the teeth on the left side of your mouth
whilst looking at yourself in the mirror, and if the bones
are not good, throw them as before saying the same words,
until you find success. As soon as you no longer see yourself in the mirror, withdraw backwards saying: *Pater, in
manus tuas, commendo spirîtum meum.* Retain this bone keep-
ing ît out of all profane sight; thereafter ît will suffice to
put ît between your teeth to render you invisible.

GARTER FOR TRAVELLING WITHOUT WEARYING

Leave the house on an empty stomach [after fasting], walk
to your left until you come across a ribbon seller and buy
one yard of white ribbon. Pay the amount he asks, letting
a farthing fall in the shop, and return home by the same
route. The next day, do the same until you come upon a
seller of feathers, buy a trimmed one – in the same way
that you bought the ribbon – and when you are at home,
write in your own blood the characters:

Figure 13

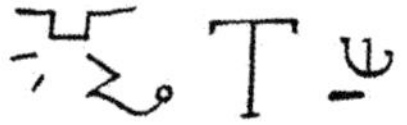

for the right garter, and these for the left garter:

Figure 14

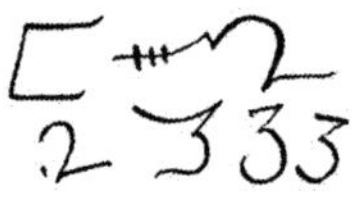

That done, leave the house on the third day wearing your ribbon and your feather; walk to the left until you find a patisserie or a bakery and buy a cake or a loaf for 2 farthings. Then go to the first cabaret you find and order a half pint of wine, have the glass rinsed three times by the same person, break into three the cake or the loaf of bread, and put the three pieces into the glass with the wine: take the first piece and throw it under the table, saying, without looking at it: *Irly, for you*; then write on the other second piece and throw it likewise saying: *Terly, for you*; then, write on the other side of the garter, with your blood, the name of these two spirits. Throw the third piece saying: *Firly, for you*; throw the feather, drink the wine without eating, pay the bill and leave. Once outside the town, put on the garters taking care not to deceive yourself by putting that meant for the right on the left and *vice versa*. This is of consequence! Stamp the ground three times with your feet, calling the names of the spirits: *Irly, Terly, Firly, Balthazar, Melchior, Gaspard, let's walk!* Then make your journey.

TO NOT GROW WEARY WHILE WALKING

Write on three silk ribbons: *Gaspar, Melchior, Balthazar*, and attach one of these ribbons below the right knee, without tightening it, the second, below the left knee, and the third about the waist. Before you set out, swallow a small glass of anise in broth or in white wine, and rub your feet with dust from the street steeped in olive oil.

TO PREVENT EATING AT THE TABLE

Plant under the table a needle which has been used to inter a corpse, and which has penetrated the flesh, then say: *Coridal, Nardac, Degon.* Afterwards place a piece of asafœtida on a burning coal and leave.

TO WIN AT GAMBLING

Pick, on the Eve of St. Peter[36] before the sun rises, the herb called *Morsus Diaboli;*[37] place it for one day on the altar stone and afterwards let it dry; grind it into a powder and carry it on you in a bag of white silk. When gathering the herb it it is necessary to make a semi-circle, with the names and cross marked in figure 15.

Figure 15

TO WIN AT THE GAME OF DICE

Dice, I conjure you in the name of Assizer and of Rassize who come to raid and loot in the names of Assa and Lengrio. Please note that you must be wearing the scapular made of clover leaves, as stated hereafter.

TO WIN AT GAMING

In stormy weather, pick clover of 4 or 5 leaves, making over it the sign of the cross, then say: *Small or large clover, I pick you in the name of the Father, and of the Son, and of the Holy Spirit, by the virginity of the Holy Virgin, by the virginity of St. John the Baptist, by the virginity of St. John the Evangelist, that you must serve me in all gambling.*

It is necessary to say afterwards five *Our Fathers* and five *Hail Marys*, then continue: *El, Aglos, Ischiros, Athanatos.* You enclose this clover in a sachet of black silk that you wear on you as a scapular, every time you play. Outside of those times, take precaution to conceal it carefully.

TO WIN EVERY TIME ON LOTTERIES

Before going to sleep, you must recite the following Orison three times, after which you place it under your pillow – written on virgin parchment over which a Mass of the Holy Spirit has been said – and during sleep, the genius of your Planet will come to you to tell you the hour in which to buy your lottery ticket.

Orison

Domine Jesus-Criste, qui dixisti: ergo sum via, verîtas, et vîta; ecce enim verîtatem dilexisti, incerta et occulta sapientae tuoe manîf-esta mihi adhuc quoe revelet in hoc nocte sicut îta revelatum fuît pervulis solis, incognîta et ventura unaque alia me doceas, ut possim omnia cognocere; si et si sît; îta monstra mihi mortem ornatam omni cibo bono, pulchrum et gratum pomarium, aut quamdam rem gratam: sin autem ministra mihi ignem ardentem, vel aquarum currentem, vel aliam quamcumque rem quoe Domino placeant, et vel Angeli, Ariel, Rubiel et Barachiel sîtis mihi mulrum amatores et jactores ad opus istud obtinendum quod cupio scire, videre, cogno-scere, et proevidere per illum Deum qui venturus est judicare vîvos et mortuos, et soeculum per ignem. Amen.

Say three *Our Fathers* and three *Hail Marys*, for the souls in purgatory.

TO BE LOVED

Draw your blood on a Friday in Spring, put it into a small new varnished earthenware pot, with the testicles of a hare and the liver of a dove, and dry it all in an oven where bread is made. Reduce it to a fine powder which you make the person upon whom you have designs swallow, about the quantity of a demi-dram (1½ grammes), and if the effect does not follow the first time, try it again up to three times, and you will be loved.

TO MAKE A GIRL COME WHOM YOU FIND TO BE SO MODEST
Experiment of a Marvelous Force of the Superior Intelligences

A star should be observed, at the crescent [waxing] or the waning of the Moon, between eleven o'clock and midnight; but before beginning, do as follows: take virgin parchment and write upon it the name of the one you wish to make come to you. It will be necessary to crop the parchment in the way shown in figure 16. The two *N*s mark the place for the names. On the other side write these words: *Machidael Barofchas*, then you put your parchment on the ground, the name of the person(s) against the earth, the right foot above and the left knee against the ground. While looking at the brilliant star, and taking hold of a candle of white wax with the right hand, which can burn for one hour, say the following conjuration:

Conjuration

I salute and conjure you, oh beautiful moon and beautiful star, brilliant light that I hold in my hand, by the air which I breathe, by the air which is in me and by the earth which I touch. I conjure you, by all the names of the Spirits, princes who preside in you, by the name

*of the ineffable who has created all, by you good Angel Gabriel with
the prince Mercury, Michael and Melchidael. I conjure you anew, by
all of the divine names of God, that you send to obsess, to torment,
to work the body, the spirit, the soul and the five senses and nature
of N, (name of the one desired) whose name is written below, that
she will come to me (name yourself), and that she will accomplish
my will and that she will have no amity for anyone in the world, especially for N as long as she remains indifferent to me, she will only
be able to endure so being obsessed, suffering and tormented. Come
then quickly, Melchidael, Bareschas, Zazel, Tiriel, Malcha, and all
those who are under you; I conjure you by the great living God, to
swiftly send her to accomplish my will. I, N promise to satisfy you.*

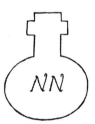

Figure 16

After having delivered this conjuration three times, put
the candle on the parchment and let it burn; the next day,
take the aforementioned parchment and put it in your left
shoe where you leave it until the person for whom you
have done the operation comes to find you.

It must be specified, in the conjuration, the day you wish
her to come and she will not miss it.

TO MAKE A GIRL DANCE COMPLETELY NUDE

Write on virgin parchment the characters in figure 17 with
bat's blood, then put that on an altar stone so that a mass
is said over it. After which, when you wish to make use of
it place this character under the doorstep where the person must pass. Scarcely will she have crossed this, than you
will see her enter in a frenzy and undress herself, and she
will dance completely nude to the death – if the character
is not removed – with grimaces and contortions which will
inspire more pity than lust.

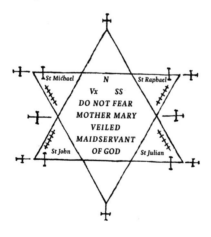

Figure 17

TO PREVENT COPULATION

For this experiment you must have a new penknife, then
on a Saturday, at the precise hour of the rising of the
Moon, in its waning phase, you will draw with the point,
behind the door where the persons sleep, the characters
in fig. 18, as well as the words: *Consummatum est*,[38] and you
break the point of the knife in the door.

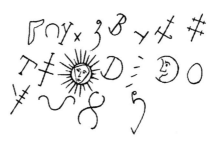

Figure 18

TO NOT BE WOUNDED BY ANY WEAPON

Say three times in the morning when you rise and at night
when you sleep: *I awaken (or I go to sleep) in the name of Jesus Christ who was crucified for me; Jesus wishes to bless me; Jesus
wishes to guide me; Jesus wishes to protect me; Jesus wishes to govern and lead me to eternal life, in the name of the Father, and of the
Son, and of the Holy Spirit.* Write upon the sword or weapon
which you wish to serve you the following: *Ibel, Ebel, Abel.*

AGAINST A SWORD-CUT

Before you go to fight, write on a ribbon of any color the two words: *Buoni jacum*. Tie your right wrist with this ribbon, defend yourself and the sword of your enemy will not touch you.

FOR GOING INTO BATTLE

Say five *Our Fathers* and five *Hail Marys* in honor of the five wounds of Our Lord, then three times say that which follows: *I go in the shirt of Our Lady, that I may be enfolded by the wounds of my God, by the four crowns of the heavens, my Lord St. John the Evangelist, Saint Luke, Saint Matthew and Saint Mark; that they will be able to protect me; that neither man, nor woman, nor lead, nor iron, nor steel, will be able to wound me, cut me, nor break my bones, peace be to God.* Then you swallow the following words having written them on white linen: *Est princîpio, est in princîpio, est un verbum, Deum est tu phantu.* It is to be done 24 hours prior to battle.

AGAINST FIREARMS

Star which guides the weapon today [ruling planet], *I charm you, I say to you, that you obey me, in the name of the Father, and of the Son, and Satanatis.* Make a sign of the cross.

TO CHARM FIREARMS

It is necessary to say whilst taking the firearm: *God has a share in this and the Devil leaves it.* Then take aim, in crossing the left leg over the right, from the prone rifle position lying down and saying in Latin: *Non tradas Dominum nostrum Jesum Christum. Mathon. Amen.*

TO MAKE A WEAPON FAIL

Take a new earthen pipe and cover its opening with brass, fill it with a root of powdered mandrake, then blow into the other end of the pipe, pronouncing at the same time: *Ablar Got, Batar Bata Bleu.*

THE HAND OF GLORY

ULL OUT THE HAIR, with its root, from a mare in heat, the closest to nature, saying: *Dragne, Dragne.*[39] Conceal this hair. Go at once to buy a new earthenware pot with its lid, without haggling. Return home with it, fill this pot with water from a fountain to within two fingers from the top, and put the aforesaid hair within; cover the pot and put it in a place where neither you nor others can see it, for that would be dangerous. After nine days, and at the same hour that you hid it, uncover the pot; you will find within it a small animal in the form of a serpent, which will raise itself upright and after which you say immediately: *I accept the pact.* That done, you take it without touching it with your hand, and put it in a new box bought expressly without haggling. You give him some wheat, nothing else, and do not forget to give him some every day.

When you want to have silver or gold, put as much as you would like to have of it in the box, and lie on your bed, placing your box near you: sleep, if you wish, for three or four hours and after this time you will find the money you had put there has doubled, but take care to replace therein the same amount.

Note that the small figure in the form of the serpent comes only by the power of the spell, and that you cannot put more than one hundred pounds at a time with him. If, however, your planet gives you power over supernatural matters, the serpent will have a face resembling that of a human, and you can then give him up to a thousand pounds; each day you reap the doubled part.

If you wish to dispose of it you can give it to whom you wish, provided that it is accepted. Otherwise, trace the signs and characters in figure 19 on virgin parchment that you place in the box, and give it to a small animal, in lieu of its usual meal of grain, over which a priest has said his first Mass, and he will die. Take good care not to forget a single circumstance, as this is no laughing matter.

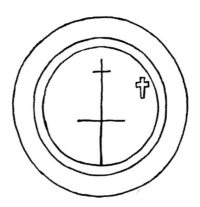

Figure 19

THE BLACK HEN

AKE A BLACK HEN which has never lain eggs and not been approached by a single cockerell. Do so in such a way that in taking her you do not make her cry out, and for this you are to go at eleven o'clock at night while she is sleeping, take her by the neck, holding it tight enough only to prevent her from crying out. Return along a road to the place where two roads cross. There, at the stroke of midnight, make a circle with a cypress wand, place yourself in the middle and rend the hen's body in two while thrice pronouncing these words: *Elohim Essaim frugativi et appellavi.*

Afterwards, turn facing towards the East, kneel and say an Orison; having done that, you make the great appellation. Then the unclean Spirit will appear to you dressed in a scarlet coat adorned with tassels, a yellow jacket and sea-green breeches. His head, which will resemble that of a dog with the ears of an ass, and will be topped by two horns; his legs and feet will be like those of a cow. He will ask your orders and you will give them to him as you see fit, for he cannot refuse to obey you, and you may make yourself the richest, and thus the happiest, of all men.

We shall say no more in this fourth part, praying only that the reader remember what we said at the beginning of this work.

THE FIFTH PART

ORISONS

ACTS OF GRACE

 lmighty God, celestial Father who has created all things for the service and the use of men, I render unto you the most humble actions of grace for that which in your great bounty you have allowed that, without risk, I can make one of your rebel spirits serve me, and accept to give me all that which I could ever need. Inspire me, oh Great God! with the necessary sentiments so that I will be able to disengage myself from the claws of the demon and all of the evil spirits. I place myself, great God the Father, God the Son, and the Holy Spirit, under your holy protection. Amen.

O Almighty Father! O Mother, the most tender of Mothers! O admirable examplary of the sentiments and the tenderness of mothers! O Son, the flower of all sons! O Form of all forms! Soul, spirit, harmony and number of all things, save us! Protect us, lead us and be propitious to us! Amen.

Now say the *Our Father* in Latin followed by the *Hail Mary*, *Ave*, in Latin, and the prayer in the Latin *Veni Creator*. End · with the *Credo*.

LATIN VERSIONS OF THE PRAYERS

Pater Noster
Pater Noster, qui es in cœlis, sanctificetur nomen tuum. Adveniat regnum tuum. Fiat voluntas tua, sicut in cœlo et in terra. Panem nostrum quotidianum da nobis hodie, et dimitte nobis debita nostra sicut et nos dimittimus debitoribus nostris. Et ne nos inducas in tentationem, sed libera nos a malo. Amen.

Ave Maria
Ave Maria, gratia plena, Dominus tecum. Benedicta tu in mulieribus, et tecum, benedicta tu in mulieribus, et benedictus fructus ventris tui Iesus. Sancta Maria, Mater Dei, ora pro nobis peccatoribus, nunc et in hora mortis nostræ. Amen.

Veni Creator

Veni, Creator Spirîtus,
mentes tuorum visîta,
imple superna gratia
quae tu creasti pectora.
Qui diceris Paraclîtus,
altissimi donum Dei,
fons vîvus, ignis, carîtas,
et spirîtalis unctio.
Tu, septiformis munere,
digîtus paternae dexterae,
Tu rîte promissum Patris,
sermone dîtans guttura.
Accende lumen sensibus:
infunde amorem cordibus:
infirma nostri corporis
virtute firmans perpeti.
Hostem repellas longius,
pacemque dones protinus:
ductore sic te prævio
vîtemus omne noxium.
Per te sciamus da Patrem,
noscamus atque Filium;
Teque utriusque Spirîtum
credamus omni tempore.
Deo Patri sît gloria,
et Filio, qui a mortuis surrexît,
ac Paraclîto, in sæculorum sæcula.
Amen.

Come, Holy Spirit, Creator blest,
and in our souls take up Thy rest;
come with Thy grace and heavenly aid
to fill the hearts which Thou hast made.
O comforter, to Thee we cry,
O heavenly gift of God Most High,
O fount of life and fire of love,
and sweet anointing from above.
Thou in Thy sevenfold gifts are known;
Thou, finger of God's hand we own;
Thou, promise of the Father,
Thou Who dost the tongue with power imbue.
Kindle our sense from above,
and make our hearts o'erflow with love;
with patience firm and virtue high
the weakness of our flesh supply.
Far from us drive the foe we dread,
and grant us Thy peace instead;
so shall we not, with Thee for guide,
turn from the path of life aside.
O may Thy grace on us bestow
the Father and the Son to know;
and Thee, through endless times confessed,
of both the eternal Spirit blest.
Now to the Father and the Son,
Who rose from death, be glory given,
with Thou, O Holy Comforter,
henceforth by all in earth and heaven.
Amen.

Symbolum Apostolorum
(I Believe In God)

Credo in Deum Patrem omnîpotentem, Creatorem caeli et terræ. Et in Iesum Christum, Filium eius unicum, Dominum nostrum, qui conceptus est de Spirîtu Sancto, natus ex Maria Virgine, passus sub Pontio Pilato, crucifixus, mortuus, et sepultus, descendît ad inferos, tertia die resurrexît a mortuis, ascendît ad cælos, sedet ad dexteram Dei Patris omnîpotentis, inde venturus est iudicare vîvos et mortuos. Credo in Spirîtum Sanctum, sanctam Ecclesiam Catholicam, sanctorum communionem, remissionem peccatorum, carnis resurrectionem, vîtam æternam. Amen.

TABLE OF FAVORABLE & UNFAVORABLE DAYS

FAVORABLE DAYS	MONTH	UNFAVORABLE DAYS
3-10-27-31	January	13-23
7-8-18	February	2-10-17-22
3-9-12-14-16	March	13-19-23-28
5-17	April	18-20-29-30
1-2-4-6-9-14	May	10-17-20
3-5-7-9-12-23	June	4-20
2-6-10-23-30	July	5-13-27
5-7-10-14-19	August	2-13-27-31
6-10-13-19-30	September	13-16-12-15
13-16-22-31	October	3-9-27
3-13-23-30	November	6-25
10-20-29	December	15-28-31

THE VERITABLE SECRET OF
THE BLACK DRAGON

BEING THE OBSERVATIONS
OF A STUDENT OF THE ART

*Comprising a truthful account
of the Frimost and Surgat Workings
by Michael Cecchetelli*

PREPARATION

Three days of preparatory work are suggested before ritual.

DAY ONE

Full physical cleaning of the temple; blessing using Abramelin oil; the Abramelin oil used to anoint myself prior to the ceremony follows the recipe given in Georg Dehn's translation: 1 part myrrh, 2 parts cinnamon, and ½ part calamus.

Progressive fast commences with meals limited to whole foods, vegetables, fruit, juices with no additives, and no animal products. Please check with a medical professional if you intend to fast in this way.

Three daily meditation sessions of 30 minutes each.

Nightly offerings to patron spirits with entreaty for their assistance in the planned rite, followed by the PGM *Headless One* rite, as adapted for my use.

DAY TWO

Physical temple and altar set up, avoid all outside influences & unimportant conversation, to remain focused. The circle in which I conducted this rite, and the majority of my workings is drawn with natron, it being the protective element par excellence for the Græco-Egyptian magus. While naturally occurring, natron is to be found only rarely outside of Khemit. It is chemically composed of no more than simple bicarbonate and sodium chloride – that is, four parts baking soda to one part kosher table salt. Intake limited to fruit, vegetables and spring water.

Three meditation sessions of 30 minutes each.

Nightly offerings to patron spirits, followed by the *Headless One* rite.

DAY THREE

Begin abstinence from all outside influence; No conversation with anyone, no internet, TV, blackberry et al. A day of meditation, reading and energy work culminating in the magickal cleansing and purification of the temple using rites I have designed for this purpose. Intake limited to fruit, vegetables and spring water. All consumption stops 24 hours before the rite with the exception of spring water. Early to sleep to assure maximum rest and stamina for the next day's work.

DAY OF THE RITE

Rise well rested and prepared mentally, physically and magickally. Ritual bath using hyssop soap and the traditional formula *Asperges me EHEIEH, Hysoppo et Mundabar lavabis ... ...* Anoint myself with Abramelin oil and dress in brand new, all white vestments. Brief prayer to my own patron asking assistance in the working.

Enter the temple.

PRAXIS

I PRELIMINARY WORK

a Establish Ritual Breathing
b Energy working (Middle Pillar or similar)
c Establish the quarters
d Offering to patron & benevolent spirits
e Invocation of the Headless One

II PRELIMINARY CONJURATION

Center of the circle, facing East: *In the name of the Father, the Son and the Holy Spirit: Take Heed, come you Spirits...*

III CALLING OF THE KINGS

Conjuration of the King of the East. While lighting candle and incense at the easternmost point: *I conjure and invoke you, O powerful Magoa, King of the East...*

Conjuration of the King of the South. While lighting candle and incense at the southernmost point: *O Egym, great King of the South, I conjure and invoke you...*

Conjuration of the King of the West. While lighting candle and incense at the westernmost point: *O King Bayemon, most strong, who rules over the Western parts...*

Conjuration of the King of the North. While lighting candle and incense at the northermost point: *O Amaymon! King-Emperor of the Northern parts, I call you...*

EVOCATION OF FRIMOST

After taking ones place behind the altar, lighting the candles thereupon and igniting the incense, gaze upon the seal of Frimost intently and deeply until the seal replicates in the mind's eye, and speak the conjuration: *I conjure you Frimost, and command you by all the names by which you may be constrained and bound...*

Gazing into the obsidian mirror, continue the evocation of Frimost while projecting his seal onto the surface until contact is established. If it becomes evident that the spirit is unwilling to relent and appear, repeat the conjuration.

When the presence of Frimost is certain and two-way communication is established, after obtaining his assent to your arrangement and his oath to assist you, in addition to the stone prescribed in the *Black Dragon*, make the pledge. The offering to be made to Frimost in compensation for his assistance is a matter best decided by the practitioner himself, of course with the assent of the spirit with whom the agreement is to be made. The offering I used in the performance of this rite, the blood of the Magus spilt on the seal of Frimost, is in stark opposition to the admonition of the original editor of the *Black Dragon*.

License to depart as below:

O thou Spirit Frimost, because thou hast diligently answered unto my demands, and hast been very ready and willing to come at my call, I do here license thee to depart unto thy proper place; without causing harm or danger unto man or beast. Depart, then, I say, and be thou very ready to come at my call, being duly exorcised and conjured by the sacred rites of magic. I charge thee to withdraw peaceably and quietly, and the peace of GOD be ever continued between thee and me, As you came in power, so go in peace!

The reader will recognize the License to Depart used in this working as drawn from the *Lemegeton*, with one notable addition in the form of the statement: *as you came in power, so go in peace* which I have found to be of great value. Credit and gratitude for this go to Frater Rufus Opus.

IV BANISHING & CLEANSING OF THE TEMPLE

In my experience banishing is not always necessary and the value of this rite has been blown all the hell out of proportion. In all my years of practical magickal evocation, there have been less than a dozen occasions when I felt it necessary or wise to attempt heavy handed treatment of the spirits such as is taught in the grimoires. I have always believed that mutually beneficial partnerships, to coin a term from the business world, are far more effective in securing the cooperation and favor of the spirits than cursing them and throwing disrespectful slurs. While I am acutely aware that there do exist such spirits as fit the moniker *evil demons* who derive great pleasure from causing pain and who would love to rend the Magus limb from limb were he not shielded from it, I can also say, from experience, that when such entities are present, there is nothing in the entire corpus of the western tradition that is going to make them leave before they choose to, and no triangle of the art or circle is going to contain them. These entities are however very rarely those named in our classical grimoires, whom we now know are for the most part the beloved deities and patrons of civilizations past whose sole evil act, albeit one for which they are to be forever condemned, is not being craven to the Judeo-Christian god.

THE MAGICAL RECORD

The following pages are copied, verbatim, from my own magickal record, and represent all the entries relevant to the Frimost working above. The reader is advised to keep in mind that the writings were not intended to be shared, but rather written, sometimes in haste, to comprise parts of my own permanent journal. As such, the parts related to the present work are commingled with fragments of other entries detailing further, unrelated magickal work and aspects of my life.

Whilst I have omitted the statement of intent, purpose and goal of the Frimost working for reasons of privacy (and because those whose will and actions it was intended to force will no doubt be among the readers of *Crossed Keys*) I can attest without any measure of hesitation that

Frimost's word, in this case at least, was gold. What I can say is that Frimost's part of the work was to accomplish four separate and very specific things; A complete 180° change in the steadfast position of two people which was in stark contradiction to my Will, the removal of an apparently immovable obstacle from my path to ascent, my receipt of a certain wisdom of an arcane & occult nature that would assist me in furtherance of a long-term plan, and my receipt of a favorable decision in a certain legal matter. All four aspects of my request to Frimost were fulfilled almost immediately.

MONDAY DEC 17TH, 2007

Uneventful day, in comparison with the events of the weekend. This evening after 30 minutes meditation I used the orphic hymns to the moon in conjunction with my G.E. lunar invocation and adoration, and an offering to my guardians. I also plan to spend some further time in meditation on Selene tonight if I get in early enough to begin on a lunar hour. I've chosen Tuesday 8th January as the date I'll carry out the next evocation from B.D. I'd still like to jump ahead to Astaroth, but will defer to (name of HGA omitted) and proceed in order with Frimost being the next. If this one turns out as successful as the previous, I'll try to work the following in without waiting as long as I did following the working of LCF. This week I have to ask (name of HGA omitted) for assistance with Venusian work next Friday.

WEDNESDAY DEC 26TH, 2007

Finished writing up the structure and prep work outline
for Frimost Working with help of (name omitted). Decided to apply KISS principle and avoid putting *too* much
thought into what I can do rather easily. Will be using the
conjurations of the Kings of the cardinal points first as
they appear to be those to whom the rest are subordinate
in the BD hierarchy. Following that, I'll employ the specific conjuration of Frimost along with his BD seal/circle
and a sigil of my own creation.

FRIDAY DEC 28TH, 2007

Feeling remarkably energized and enthusiastic after the
Venusian work tonight!!! Looking forward to creating the
metallic seal of Hagith I promised, and to having further
dealings. Cherishing that rare moment at the end of a rite
when I can say I *know* it had the desired affect and the
Willed change has been made. Even before the phone rang
just now I knew I had it locked. Fucking Hagith I owe you!
Going to finish the altar design and circle for Frimost; I've
been severely overtaken by events and let Jan 8th creep up
on me. According to (name omitted) I need to get my head
in the game and stop waiting until the last minute. Think-
ing of using a simple Solomonic circle with the hexagram,
similar to the one on my medallion. Debating whether to
use a material/physical offering of blood, or whether it's
more appropriate to stick with incense. Much, much to
think about in a short time.

TUESDAY JAN 1ST 2008

Wondering if today would have been a better election for the Frimost rite? Despite the 8ᵗʰ being the date given to me by (name omitted), it just seems that the first day of a new year holds, in and of itself, some magick from which I could have drawn. Asi es, asi sera... He's never let me down yet, and it is too late to second guess. All details have been finalized, got Monday – Wednesday off and told everyone I won't be answering the phones or emails on the 7ᵗʰ or 8ᵗʰ. Alea iacta est. Beginning the fast on Saturday along with the prep work selected; between now and then I will continue my nightly planetary work. For today made a special offering to the patrons and to Anpu in particular for the insight given me in LD. Received ½ lb of sand from the foot of the Great Pyramid yesterday from a civ contractor Jim knows, who I'm sure must think I'm crazy as shit for requesting such a thing. I think Anpu, Aset, Asar and Heru will appreciate being upon the sands of their home again, even if it is in this way. Going to induce Lucid Dreaming tonight with intent to travel there using Laberge's method.

SATURDAY JANUARY 5TH, 2008

And so it begins... Enjoyed a good meal last night and as of 12:01 AM I've begun my progressive fast and other preparatory work for Tuesday's rite. Cleaned out the temple room extensively, banished all unwanted spirits and reinvited the welcomed. Began 30 × 3 meditations at 3:33 AM, along with focusing & centering work. Ended the evening with

offering to patrons and to Him, followed by 3 × *Headless
Rite* which proved far more empowering than in recent
memory, perhaps due to the pronunciation improvements
with the words of power and new technique of empow-
ered vibration given to me by (name omitted). Going to
bed reading mundane novel to relax the brain.

SATURDAY JANUARY 5TH, 2008 – SUPP.

Awakened at 11 something after very vivid lucid dream re;
Frimost work. Going to get as much of it down in the
dream journal as I can before I forget. Have to ask (name
omitted) for the significance of the panther and research if
it has been recorded as the appearance of any known spirit,
or perhaps a form taken by one in that plane. Need to research the name AMAKIEL as well as I seem to have heard it
in one grimoire list of spirits or another, hopefully can be
found in my database. Need to first determine if anything
from this dream are related to or bear on Frimost working,
and if not put them on the back burner until Wednesday
so as not to be distracted from the rite in progress.

SUNDAY JANUARY 6TH, 2008

3:33 AM meditation difficult today after staying up until
12:30 recording dreams, but I made it work despite the
exhaustion. Back to sleep around 4:30 until 10 AM with
no memorable dreams, lucid or otherwise. Spent the af-
ternoon preparing the materia magica and setting up the
temple and altar. Consecrated the natron to be used for

circle construction & created the circle with solomonic hexagram design as per *Key of Solomon*, laid out with table of practice #2 and tools, sigil of Frimost, obsidian mirror and blade. Second 30 min meditation ended up lasting 68 min, lost in my own sub c, but well worth it. Today's meals consisted solely of apples, pears, strawberries and celery with Poland Spring. Surprisingly I'm not as hungry as last time. During the evening's offering to patrons and HO the presence of Anpu was very distinct and clearly visible in the obsidian mirror which is already in place for Frimost, however no communication or dialogue occurred. Very tired this evening and after 3rd meditation session, I'm going to call it a night. Did pretty well with limitation of contact and convo; took no calls, only checked email and spoke to no one outside family.

SUNDAY JANUARY 6TH, 2008 – SUPP.

Awakened 11:30; during lucid dream, astral separation. In astral body, went to temple with intentions of making an offering of energy while OOB and hoping to establish astral contact with patrons again as past experience tells me this can prove worthwhile and beneficial since communication isn't limited. Temple was not what it should be, appeared as the chamber in abu simbel but rather than the statues and icons in my own temple, the enthroned gods were present as if holding court. I gave the traditional Khemitian sign of deference with both palms held out towards them. Only Aset spoke, something to the effect:

We guide and empower you in all things and will indwell your soul
temple when you have need of us. Seek us in Pi-Ramesses and call to
us from the Ka and the Ba, and here in this temple shall we be, but
do not be distracted or separated from your purpose, for in all works
you must place all of you. I've already recorded everything in
my dream log as well as in the book of the patrons and will
consult N to see why this has occurred since I see no paral-
lel between it and my present work. I will for the moment
take the advice given, since I interpret the be not distracted admonition as telling me to focus on what I am engaged
in, and put this experience on hold until Wednesday. The
only thing I don't understand is why Anpu did not speak
since he is the one who comes to me most frequently, and
why Aset wore neither the throne upon her head or the
horns of Hathoor.

MONDAY JANUARY 7TH, 2008

No Entry

WEDNESDAY JANUARY 9TH, 2008 — 2:35 AM
(immediately post working)

The work of Frimost is finished and went far better than
I'd hoped! During the second recitation of the BD Conjuration of Frimost, presence became clear in the surface of the
mirror with the evoked appearing in roughly humanoid
form. While the vision itself was limited to the surface
area of the mirror, the area around it took on a light grey

glow unrelated to the incense and candles. Upon appearance, I began asking the standard: *Identify yourself*, taught
in grimoires, but he interrupted with: *Why would any but the
named come when the invitation to eat at your table was so replete
with threats and intimidation? And why, if your intent is to ask
of me a gift, would you deem it acceptable and wise to promise to
torment me day after day should I not agree? I come not out of fear
nor out of obligation, for over me no man has power. I come because
you think to give me blood in exchange for what you seek, and that
I would have.* I told Frimost my purpose for calling him and
what I needed using the statement of intent I wrote out
during the conception phase; (nature of rite withheld) to
which he said: *I am well aware of your desire and what it is you
expect from me. Your intent takes shape in the astral plane when
you dream and is bare for all there to see as was your intent to ca-
jole and coerce. If it were not my intent to grant this you would not
have seen me this night despite your threats, indeed threats which
you know you should not and need not utter.* I asked Frimost to
explain, and he pointed out that in my own work I never
make use of threats or attempt to command those whom I
evoke and further scolded me for doing so now, especially
for attempting to do so using names of gods that I do not
respect (JC). He said while it is perfectly fine to seek out he
and his kind using the teachings of long dead practitioners, it would be folly to fool myself into believing that I can
command or force the obedience of those I call with names
of gods before whom they refuse to bow. He said he had
given enough time to idle banter and that I would have what I

desire, and in the future when I come before him I have to
*refrain from idle threats that none but the unseen one could hope
to enforce and approach him respectfully as one would approach an
elder.* I agreed, and using the blade I cut the ring finger on
my right hand, allowing the blood to fall onto his sigil. I
need to be sure in future work that when a blood offering
is made to the evoked, it is done only when the evocation
is into a mirror, bowl or other scrying surface and not to
physical form; the energy that came from his likeness in
the obsidian when I made this gift was frightening. Following the offering, he showed me a sign that I can use
to call him in the future. I almost began the license to depart I'd prepared and drew a fiery look from the mirror. I
changed it to: *As you came in power, so go in peace, and let there
always be peace between us*, which seemed more acceptable to
Frimost. Per his words admonishing me against *idle threats*
I refrained from any further license or commands to depart. Upon his departure I extinguished the candles and
left the temple. I took an hour to shower and eat, and now
am writing up my summary.

THE EVOCATION OF SURGAT

In my evocation of Frimost I had been advised to under-
take the operations of conjuration within the *Black Dragon*
in the order in which they are presented in the text. The
first of the two Surgat workings represents the experience
where this was revealed. While I do consider the first to
have been a successful endeavor, since two-way communi-

cation was indeed established, ît failed to yield the results
I had intended. The rîtual structure employed for the first
evocation consisted of the same preparatory work as that
of the Frimost working. It differed however, in that I did
not first call on the Kings of the Cardinal Directions. Instead, prior to the specific conjuration of Surgat, the rather
lengthy Conjuration of the Demons was used. In all sub-
sequent workings the structure outlined by Frimost was
adhered to.

SUNDAY SEPT 3RD, 2007 – EVOCATION OF SURGAT

The working is complete wîth mixed results. I did achieve
manifestation of the spirît Surgat, but the wisdom I wanted was not forthcoming. The rîte was begun as I planned
ît, including the empowering rîte. I carried out the Conjuration of the Demons perfectly, despîte îts length, from
memory and followed immediately wîth that of Surgat.
Surgat did appear after the fifth recîtation of his conjuration, but only to tell me that ît was necessary to work first
wîth those who come before him in the MS. His counte-
nance was not discernible, only the outline appeared in
the smoke, but his words were clear and he said if I had
bothered to consult N rather than just *telling* him of my
plans, he could have told me that the working outlined in
BD was in a certain order for a certain reason. Apparently
BD is intended to be worked by calling down the Kings
who rule the directions first, and in their presence summoning the rulers of each day on their day, and in order,

securing their cooperation in turn. After explaining this, Surgat departed abruptly and without ceremony. I gave the license to depart anyway, before extinguishing the candles and leaving.

SUNDAY OCT 5TH, 2008 – SECOND EVOCATION OF SURGAT

The second attempt at evoking Surgat has been largely successful, at least in securing his assent to deliver the information and wisdom I asked for. This time Surgat did appear almost immediately and responded to my request for (omitted) by pointing me to several texts which he says are far less corrupt and more historically and magickally correct than any others, having been unknown for much of their lives and thus untainted by the multitudes adding, revising and bowdlerizing. Contrary to the warning in BD, at no time did he request a hair of my head, although I'm sure someone would argue that with the blood offering made to him it would be unnecessary. Surgat appears somewhat smaller in stature than his predecessors, but speaks with great authority. Need to ask N if this and his placement as the seventh spirit evoked indicate some unknown office? Also need to research him more, and other permutations of the name he gave for calling him without full ceremony. Following the offering to him his departure was pretty anticlimactic. Following the counsel previously given by Frimost and echoed by (omitted) I left out the dramatic license to depart the same way I modified the conjurations to exclude the harsher aspects.

CLOSING REMARKS

The most vital conclusion I've drawn from my work with the *Black Dragon* is that while time and transference between many hands has tainted it, removing instructions that originally filled in the gaps and explained how the whole of the text prior to the *Spells and Counter-Spells* was intended as a single operation, it still remains a viable system. The work, as it was originally intended, consists of the evocation of the four Kings of the Cardinal directions, herein named Amaymon, Bayemon, Egym and Magoa. Following the successful evocation of the four Kings by means of *Black Dragon*'s *Conjuration of the Demons* and their individual incantations, power is conveyed upon the Magus by their combined authority over the whole of the infernal kingdom to then summon those who rule the days of the week in their name. This is what was meant by Frimost when he alluded to the fact that summoning him in the name of the Christian god was not the means by which he is compelled, as he owes no loyalty or obedience to him. The secret of the *Black Dragon*, as explained by encountering those who grace its pages, is that despite its pretenses to work its magick in the name of the Abrahamic god, thus making it less offensive and heretical to anyone who happens upon it, it is in truth a means by which one may use the power of the highest of the infernal spirits, in this case the four Kings, to summon and enlist the aid of their subordinates, and through them to affect practical and tangible change in the world.

This revelation shows that the source of the *Black Dragon*'s power and its value is not in the pseudo-pious verbiage of the conjurations, but the formula concealed beneath them. The concept of compelling one spirit to obey or to appear by means of the authority and name of its superior is one found in a plethora of the grimoires as well as modern works, both infernal and celestial. I do not assert that in all such works, wherein the names of the heavenly host are used to summon the infernal, that the same rule applies; simply that it is indeed the case here as proven to me by my own work with the text. I have, over a period of a year, carried out all seven evocations, obtaining piece after piece of the puzzle that is *Black Dragon*, until finally, following the second conjuration of Surgat, I undertook to evoke all seven rulers in one ceremony wherein the whole of the mystery was revealed. I submit these findings and results, along with excerpts from my own magickal record, only as a testament to what holds as truth for me, and me alone. It is my wish that they spark within you the desire to investigate, research, discuss and most importantly of all, experience this art of Magick for yourself.

THE ENCHIRIDION
OF POPE LEO III

Orisons & Secrets
Illustrated with
Mystical Seals
and Figures

TO THE WISE CABALISTS

 NLY AFTER assiduous and demand-
ing researches have we managed to
perfect and complete the *Enchiridion
of Pope Leon*. All the different im-
prints of this work of which we
are in possession, such as those
of Parma, Mainz, Ancona, Rome,
Lyon & Frankfurt etc., have placed
us in the position of presenting it to the Curious with more
order and accuracy than has hitherto appeared. The method of making use of it varies in nearly all editions of the
Work, and it is perhaps on account of these various chang-
es, or because some analogy was found with the name of
the Author, that he has been called the PAPILLON.[1] We find
in the different editions of this Book, the seven psalms, to
which we have added their virtues with the character and
the name of the spirit they refer to, taken from the Cabala.
Charlemagne, to whom this Work is consecrated, as an
offering and a precious treasure, was the first to know of

its surprising and marvelous effects, through experience; he devoutly recited the Orisons, his face turned towards the rising Sun, and vowed to carry them on himself, written in gold letters: all the figures with which the Book is illustrated are drawn from the most rare manucripts that antiquity has bequeathed to us, and they are bound to the Orisons where they are found; they operate by being worn or carried on oneself. One can consult, on their subject, the *Magical Calendar of Occult Philosophy* of the celebrated Agrippa.

See note 2, page 210

100

IN THE BEGINNING
ACCORDING TO THE GOSPEL OF JOHN

*N THE BEGINNING was the Word, and the Word was with God, and the Word was God. It began with God. All things have been made by Him, nothing that has been made was made without Him. In Him was life, and His life was the light of men. And this Light shone in the darkness, and the darkness could not penetrate it. There was a man sent by God, whose name was John, who came as a witness to give testimony of the Light, so all would believe. He was not the Light; but he came to bear witness to the Light. That was the true Light that illuminates every man come into this world. He was in the world, and the world was made by Him, and the world knew Him not. He came unto his own, and his own did not receive Him. But he gave the power to be children of God to all those who received Him, to those who believed in His name, who were born not of blood, nor of the will of the flesh, nor the will of man, but of God Himself. And the Word was made flesh, and dwelt among us: and we beheld His glory, glory as of the only Son of the Father, filled with Grace and with the Truth. Let us give thanks to God. Hosanna, salvation and glory to the Son of God. Blessed are they who come in the name of the Lord. O king of Israel, hosanna, salvation and glory in heaven.*

*By that which you bring forth always, Lord, you sanctify, you en-
liven, you bless and you bestow on us these gifts; it is by virtue of
Him and with Him that all honour and all glory belong. To God the
Father Almighty, in unity with the Holy Spirit through all time. So
be it. Let us pray. Instructed by salutary commandments, and following the divine rule given us by Jesus Christ, we dare to say: Our
Father who art in heaven...*

This psalm gives the power to be made children of God
to all those who believe in Him, and believe in His name,
who were not born of blood, nor of the desires of the flesh,
nor of the will of man, but of God, being regenerated by
the Sacrament, and by the grace of Jesus Christ.

PSALM 6

Domine, ne in furore tuo arguas me ...

*O Lord, rebuke me not in thine anger, neither chasten me in thy
displeasure. Have mercy upon me, O Lord, for I am weak! O Lord,
heal me, for my bones are vexed. My soul is sore and vexed: O Lord,
how long? Return, O Lord, and deliver my soul! Oh save me, for thy
mercies' sake. For in death there is no remembrance of thee: in the
grave who shall give thee thanks? I am weary with my groaning:
all the night make I my bed to swim; I water my couch with my
tears. Mine eye is consumed because of grief; it waxeth old because
of all mine enemies. Depart from me, all ye workers of iniquity; for
the Lord hath heard the voice of my weeping. The Lord hath heard*

my supplication; the Lord will receive my prayer. Let all mine enemies be ashamed and sore vexed: let them return and be ashamed suddenly.

David wrote this Psalm to ask God for victory over his son, Absalom, and forgiveness for his sins. If it is said with devotion, it comforts the sinner, and removes the sadness of having offended God, and converts it into joy and love.

Saint Cassiodorus says that those who devoutly say this Psalm three times in succession will change the ill will of an unjust Judge, and prevents a wrongful conviction.

It is good against all works and torments of the spirit, saying it seven times in the course of the day when one needs, each time calling the name of its Intelligence, then say: *I beg you ISU, Lord of Salvation by virtue of your holy names and of this Psalm, may you free me, N, from the torments and the evil of which you can deliver as it pleases you.*

This psalm is good against ills of the eye, if said seven times a day over three consecutive days, naming the Intelligence at the end, and each time writing the character on a lettuce leaf, with which you must touch the eye. The name of the Intelligence is **Hael**, and his character is:

PSALM 31
Beati quorum remissæ sunt ...

In thee, O Lord, do I put my trust; let me never be ashamed: deliver me in thy righteousness. Bow down thine ear to me; deliver me speedily: be thou my strong rock, for a house of defense to save me. For thou art my rock and my fortress; therefore for thy name's sake lead me, and guide me. Pull me out of the net they have laid for me: for thou art my strength. Into thine hand I commit my spirit: thou hast redeemed me, O Lord God of truth. I have hated them that regard lying vanities: but I trust in the Lord. I will be glad and rejoice in thy mercy: for thou hast considered my trouble; thou hast known my soul in adversities.

And hast not shut me up into the hand of the enemy: thou hast set my feet in a large room. Have mercy on me, O Lord, for I am in trouble: mine eye is consumed with grief, yea, my soul and my belly. For my life is spent with grief, and my years with sighing: my strength faileth because of mine iniquity, and my bones are consumed. I was a reproach among all mine enemies, but especially among my neighbors, and a fear to mine acquaintances: they that did see me without fled from me. I am forgotten as a dead man out of mind; I am like a broken vessel. For I have heard the slander of many: fear was on every side: while they took counsel together against me, they devised to take away my life. But I trusted in thee, O Lord: I said, Thou art my God. My times are in thy hand: deliver me from the hand of mine enemies, and from them that persecute me. Make thy face to shine upon thy servant: save me for thy mer-

cies' sake. Let me not be ashamed, O Lord; for I have called upon
thee: let the wicked be ashamed, and let them be silent in the grave.
Let the lying lips be put to silence; which speak grievous things
proudly and contemptuously against the righteous. Oh how great
is thy goodness, which thou hast laid up for them that fear thee;
which thou hast wrought for them that trust in thee before the sons
of men. Thou shalt hide them in the secret of thy presence from the
pride of man: thou shalt keep them secretly in a pavilion from the
strife of tongues. Blessed be the Lord; for he hath showed me his
marvelous kindness in a strong city. For I have said in my haste, I
am cut off from before thine eyes; nevertheless thou heardest the
voice of my supplications when I cried unto thee. O love the Lord, all
ye his saints: for the Lord preserveth the faithful, and plentifully re-
wardeth the proud doer. Be of good courage, and he shall strengthen
your heart, all ye that hope in the Lord.

The Luminaries

This Psalm is used to know whether God has forgíven our sins; and ít counters the bítes of dogs and snakes, and particularly the verse, *in camo et freno*, etc... It is good also for those who have hidden secrets and crimes, and fear being discovered, if ít is said three times every day as long as there is fear that the secret will be dívulged, wíth the name of the Intelligence which must be wrítten on one's chest, wíth íts charaćter, and ít will not be śpoken of. The Intelligence's name is **Hunel**. The charaćter is:

PSALM 37
Domine, ne in furore tuo arguas me ...

Fret not thyself because of evil-doers, neíther be thou envious against the workers of iniquíty. For they śhall soon be cut down like the grass, and wíther as the green herb. Trust in the Lord, and do good; so śhalt thou dwell in the land, and verily thou śhalt be fed. Delight thyself also in the Lord; and he śhall gíve thee the desires of thine heart. Commít thy way unto the Lord; trust also in him; and he śhall bring ít to pass. And he śhall bring forth thy righteousness as the light, and thy judgment as the noonday. Rest in the Lord, and waít patiently for him: fret not thyself because of him who prospereth in his way, because of the man who bringeth wićked devices to pass. *Cease from anger, and forsake wrath; fret not thyself in any wise to do evil. For evildoers ſhall be cut off: but those that waìt upon the Lord, they ſhall inherìt the earth. For yet a lìttle while, and the wicked ſhall not be: yea thou ſhalt diligently consider his place, and ìt ſhall not be. But the meek ſhall inherìt the earth, and ſhall delight themselves in the abundance of peace. The wicked plotteth against the just, and gnaſheth upon him wìth his teeth. The Lord ſhall laugh at him: for he seeth that his day is coming. The wicked have drawn out the sword, and have bent their bow, to cast down the poor and needy, and to slay ſuch as be of upright conversation. Their sword ſhall enter into their own heart, and their bows ſhall be broken. A lìttle that a righteous man hath is better than the riches of many wicked. For the arms of the wicked ſhall be broken: but the Lord upholdeth the righteous. The Lord knoweth the days of the upright: and their inherìtance ſhall be forever.*

They ſhall not be aſhamed in the evil time: and in the days of famine they ſhall be satisfied. But the wicked ſhall periſh, and the enemies of the Lord ſhall be as the fat of lambs: they ſhall consume; into smoke ſhall they consume away. The wicked borroweth, and payeth not again: but the righteous ſhoweth mercy, and gìveth. For ſuch as be blessed of him ſhall inherìt the earth; and they that be cursed of him ſhall be cut off. The steps of a good man are ordered by the Lord: and he delighteth in his way. Though he fall, he ſhall not be utterly cast down: for the Lord upholdeth him wìth his hand. I have been young, and now am old; yet have I not seen the righteous forsaken, nor his seed begging bread. He is ever merciful, and lendeth; and his seed is blessed. Depart from evil, and do good; and dwell forevermore. For the Lord loveth judgment, and forsaketh not

his saints; they are preserved forever: but the seed of the wicked
shall be cut off. The righteous shall inherit the land, and shall dwell
therein forever. The mouth of the righteous speaketh wisdom, and
his tongue talketh of judgment. The law of his God is in his heart;
none of his steps shall slide. The wicked watcheth the righteous, and
seeketh to slay him. The Lord shall not leave him in his hand, nor
condemn him when he is judged. Wait on the Lord, and keep his
way, and he shall exalt thee to inherit the land: when the wicked are
cut off, thou shalt see it.

I have seen the wicked in great power, and spreading himself
like a green bay tree. Yet he passed away, and, lo, he was not: yea I
sought him, but he could not be found. Mark the perfect man, and
behold the upright; for the end of that man is peace. But the trans-
gressors shall be destroyed together: the end of the wicked shall be
cut off. But the salvation of the righteous is of the Lord: he is their
strength in the time of trouble. And the Lord shall help them, and
deliver them: he shall deliver them from the wicked, and save them,
because they trust in him.

Saint Jerome and Saint Augustine assure us that one
who says this Psalm with devotion obtains remission of
his sins, and exempts him from the punishment he de-
serves. It cures epilepsy or falling sickness, if one writes
it with a stylus on a silver blade, when Mars is in good
aspect with the Moon. The name and character of the Intelligence must be written, along with the character and
Intelligence of Tuesday, and it should be said to the patient
in the morning and evening for seven consecutive days.

He should wear the aforesaid blade around his neck during that time. The Intelligence's name is **Ramiach**, and the
character is:

PSALM 50
Miserere mei, Deus, secundum magnam ...

The mighty God, even the Lord, hath spoken, and called the earth
from the rising of the sun unto the going down thereof. Out of Zion,
the perfection of beauty, God hath shined. Our God shall come, and
shall not keep silence: a fire shall devour before him, and it shall
be very tempestuous round about him. He shall call to the heavens
from above, and to the earth, that he may judge his people. Gather
my saints together unto me; those that have made a covenant with
me by sacrifice. And the heavens shall declare his righteousness: for
God is judge himself. Selah. Hear, O my people, and I will speak; O
Israel, and I will testify against thee: I am God, even thy God. I will
not reprove thee for thy sacrifice or thy burnt offerings, to have been
continually before me. I will take no bullock out of thy house, nor he
goats out of thy folds: For every beast of the forest is mine, and the
cattle upon a thousand hills. I know all the fowls of the mountains:
and the wild beasts of the field are mine. If I were hungry, I would
not tell thee: for the world is mine, and the fullness whereof. Will
I eat the flesh of bulls, or drink the blood of goats? Offer unto God

*thanksgiving; and pay thy vows unto the Most High: And call upon
me in the day of trouble: I will deliver thee, and thou shalt glorify
me. But unto the wicked God saith, what hast thou to do to declare
my statutes, or that thou shouldst take my covenant in thy mouth?
Seeing thou hatest instruction, and castest my words behind thee.
When thou sawest a thief, then thou consented with him, and hast
been partaker with adulterers. Thou givest thy mouth to evil, and
thy tongue frameth deceit. Thou sittest and speakest against thy
brother; thou slanderest thine own mother's son. These things hast
thou done, and I kept silence; thou thoughtest that I was altogether
such a one as thyself; but I will reprove thee, and set them in order
before thine eyes. Now consider this, ye that forget God, lest I tear
you in pieces, and there be none to deliver. Whoso offereth praise
glorifieth me: and to him that ordereth his conversation aright will
I show the salvation of God.*

Having taken Bathsheba after the death of her husband
Uriah, and the prophet Nathan having taken her again, as
seen in the second book of *Kings*, chapter 12, David knowing then his sin wrote this Psalm which has the virtue to
give contrition: he composed it by the command of God.

Saint Jerome says it will give remission of our sins, if
one says it every day since they were committed. Saint
Augustine says our sins will be forgiven and we will as-
cend to Heaven, which makes this prayer admirable. Saint
Ambrose calls it the glorious Psalm, useful for the health
of body and soul, when said every day. It counters temptations if one says it three times a day over linseed oil,

and with this oil mark the character over one's heart. The
name of the Intelligence is **Jendsel**. The character is:

PSALM 101
Domine, exaudi orationem meam ...

*I will sing of mercy and judgment: unto thee, O Lord, will I sing. I
will behave myself wisely in a perfect way. O when wilt thou come
unto me? I will walk within my house with a perfect heart. I will set
no wicked thing before mine eyes: I hate the work of them that turn
aside; it shall not cleave to me. A froward heart shall depart from
me: I will not know a wicked person. Whoso privily slandereth his
neighbor, him will I cut off: him that hath a high look and a proud
heart I will not suffer. Mine eyes shall be upon the faithful of the
land, that they may dwell with me: he that walketh in a perfect
way, he shall serve me. He that worketh deceit shall not dwell within
my house: he that telleth lies shall not tarry in my sight. I will early
destroy all the wicked of the land; that I may cut off all wicked doers
from the city of the Lord.*

David made this Psalm for the people of Israel, who were
to be delivered by the coming of Jesus Christ, as it is written in the second book of *Macabees*. This should be the sev-

enth of the Penitential Psalms, with reason. Saint Jerome guarantees that whoever says it devoutly everyday will be wondrously consoled in all his afflictions. To make a barren woman conceive, it is necessary to write with devotion the Intelligence and character on white taffeta, all with the blood of a dove, and the woman must wear it around the neck always. And when she lies with her husband, she must not fail to turn it behind her, to hang between her shoulder blades so it lies along her spine. The name of the Intelligence is **Silti** or **Silli**, and this is the character:

PSALM 125
De profundis clamavi ad te, Domine ...

They that trust in the Lord shall be as Mount Zion, which cannot be removed, but abideth forever. As the mountains are round about Jerusalem, so the Lord is round about his people from henceforth even forever. For the rod of the wicked shall not rest upon the lot of the righteous; lest the righteous put forth their hands unto iniquity. Do good, O Lord, unto those that be good, and to them that be upright in their hearts. As for such that turn aside unto their crooked ways, the Lord shall lead them forth with the workers of iniquity: but peace shall be upon Israel.

This Psalm of the second degree was sung, figuring that the Church of God prays incessantly for sinners, in order to erase the stains of their crimes. Saint Jerome says that David was converted by its virtue, as was the apostle Saint Paul, and the people of God delivered. Saint Augustine calls this Orison truly penitential, because it is useful for the dead, above all the other psalms. It is good against storms and against temptations, and the same Saint says that this prayer has always been answered by God, when it has been said with devotion.

It is used to give revelations in dreams, if one writes the Intelligence and character on three cedar leaves that are then put under the pillow when retiring to bed, and the Psalm is said three times, and thrice is said: *I pray Hassar, that you show me clearly tonight, the answer of what I desire to know.* The name of the Intelligence is **Stilu**, and the character is:

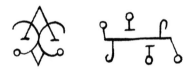

PSALM 142
Domine, exaudi orationem meam ...

I cried unto the Lord with my voice; with my voice unto the Lord did I make my supplication. I poured out my complaint before him; I showed before him my trouble. When my spirit was overwhelmed within me, then thou knewest my path. In the way wherein I walked have they laid a snare for me. I looked upon my right hand, and beheld, but there was no man that would know me: refuge failed me; no man cared for my soul. I cried unto thee, O Lord: I said, Thou art my refuge and my portion in the land of the living. Attend unto my cry; for I am brought very low: deliver me from my persecutors; for they are stronger than I. Bring my soul out of prison, that I may praise thy name: the righteous shall compass me about; for thou shalt deal bountifully with me.

To be used as an instruction. God told David that he would never be delivered from his enemies and that he would never come into his kingdom, had he not made this Psalm, which is called the *Lachrymose Orison of David*, by virtue of which he achieved all that he had asked; for the Holy Spirit guided him in all his actions. Its virtue leads us by the spirit of God in all glorious places filled with spiritual and temporal goods. Saint Jerome says that it procures the salvation of body and soul above all other Psalms. It is penitential and of great virtue. It is good for travelers by land and sea, and for those who seek offices and dignities; if they are good people, the Holy Spirit will show them the way they must follow and will preserve them on the days they say it. Saint Jerome confirms having experimented with several others. It is good for those who wish to withdraw from the world, or marry, or succeed in all things, because the Holy Spirit will lead them by the virtue of

this Psalm. It is also useful for prisoners, doing what is
prescribed in Psalm 141.

Note that it is not necessary to persuade the impious,
the incredulous, mockers, the grandiose, the miserly, li-
ars, and other sinners, or those enclosed in the darkness
of vice, ignorance, and all the other human passions, that
they can taste the fruits of a divine tree; for if an inquisi-
tive person wanted to experience it to satisfy his curiosity,
his pleasure, his revenge, his avarice, his vanity and other
passions, and if it fails to accord with his desires, he must
not attribute the fault to this holy work, but only to himself, rendered unworthy by his crimes; because this grace,
so admirable and so particular, is reserved only for those
who are truly good, and full of charity, piety, humility, and
all the other divine virtues.

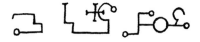

THE ENCHIRIDION
OF POPE LEO III

A rare gift & correspondence from His Serenity,
in the Vatican, to the Holy Emperor, Charlemagne.

 OLY POPE LEO III assembled and put in order the following Orisons of the words and precepts of our holy Mother Church and sent it to Charlemagne, saying: *If you firmly believe, without question, that each day you devoutly recite the following Orison, and carry it reverently with you, whether in the house, or in war, or upon the sea, or wheresoever you are, none of your enemies will have advantage over you; you will be invincible, and delivered of the most wicked defects and all adversities. In the name of Our Lord Jesus Christ. Amen.*

In memory of King Charlemagne, this was written in gold letters, which he always wore on himself with great care and with the utmost respect and devotion.

No mortal can express the virtues of this Orison. If men knew its excellence and virtue, they would recite it every day with great devotion, and would never cease from carrying a copy on them, especially since there is no-one in the world who, having recited it, has been abandoned by God in all his needs and necessities, and having come to its end, finishing his days happily. This undeniable experience was made known to many, as whosoever recites it devoutly every day and carries it on him with honour and respect, without any change to their body, for the glory and praise of God almighty, for the glorious Virgin Mary His Mother, and for all the heavenly Court, will be preserved from iron, water, fire, and sudden death. Even the Devil will have no power over him; nor will he die without confession, neither while sleeping, nor on or off the path, nor in any place that he may be. He will never be overcome, nor be made captive. The Orison is marvelous against tempests, lightning and thunder. If one recites it over holy water, with which one asperges the air in the shape of a cross, storms and thunder immediately cease. If one is at sea and recites it three times, there will be no distressing accidents nor storm on that day. If it is said three times over a person possessed by an evil spirit, by the light of a blessed candle, he will be delivered straight away.

If a woman is in danger during the labour of childbirth, recíte the Orison three times holding a lighted blessed candle, and she will be delívered at once. If someone wants to go on a journey, he should recíte ît three times before leaving and carry ît on himself always, for the duration of the voyage, and he will be delívered from any accident or sin, and if he comes to die of some disease, he will be saved. These trustworthy Orisons have been proved by many people.

Here begin the mysterious Orisons of Pope Leo III.

THE ORISONS OF WHICH THE MAGICIAN
MAY AVAIL HIMSELF

ORISON AGAINST ALL KINDS OF CHARMS,

enchantments, spells, characters (sigils & talismans), visions, illusions, possessions, obsessions, malefic obstruction of marriage, & all that can happen to us through the evil spells of sorcerers, or by incursions of devils; and it is also beneficial against all kinds of misfortune that can be directed against horses, mares, oxen, cows, sheep, ewes, & other species of animal.

ORD WHICH WAS MADE FLESH, nailed to a cross, and who sits at the right hand of the Father, I entreat you by your holy Name, at the utterance of which all genuflect, grant the prayers of those who put their confidence and belief in you, and by the merits of the Blessed Virgin Mary, and by the prayers of all the Saints of God, deign to preserve this creature, N, from all those who would harm, and from attacks by demons or malignant spirits, you who live and reign with God the Father and the Holy Spirit, Three as One in perfect unity; for the cross of our Lord Jesus Christ, upon which we depend for our salvation, our life, our resurrection, and the confounding of the evil spirits and all those who seek to harm us.

119

Thus, flee from here, disappear, my enemies, cursed men; for I banish you, infernal demons and wicked spirits no matter what type you be, present or absent, in any manner whatsoever it be, or under any pretext whatsoever, whether you have been invoked or sent, be it out of good will, or by compulsion; be it by enchantment, or the art of evil men, or of women; you hasten to remain or vex. Until you quit your diabolical trickery, going anywhere without restraint, by the great living God ✠ by the True God ✠ by the Holy God ✠ by God the Father ✠ by God the Son ✠ and by the Holy Spirit, who is also God ✠ but especially by He ✠ who was sacrificed as Isaac ✠ sold as Joseph ✠ who was crucified as a man ✠ who suffered and was killed as a lamb, by the blood of Saint Michael, who fought with you, and, leading the victory, overcame you and forced you to withdraw. You will not, under any pretext whatsoever, be able to molest or torment this creature, neither in or out of its body, neither by vision, nor by fright, nor during the day nor by night, neither in sleep, nor waking, neither whilst eating, praying or doing any natural or spiritual act: otherwise I will cast upon you curses, maledictions and excommunications, condemning you, at the hands of your enemies, at the behest of the Holy Trinity, and executed by the Archangel Michael, to be hurled into the lake of fire and sulphur.

For if you previously took some bond of adoration and worship, some perfume, some fine and malign attachment, be it herbs, or words, or stones, or elements; whether they are natural or simple or mixed, or whether temporal, or spiritual, or sacramental, or in the name of the Great God, or the Angels, whether they are in the characters of the hours, of minutes, of days, of the year, and of the month, observed superstitiously with pact uttered, or tacit, even

strengthened by solemn oath. I break, destroy, and cancel all these
things, by the power and virtue of God the Father ✚ who has cre-
ated all things. By the wisdom of God the Son ✚ Redeemer of men.
And by the bounty of the Holy Spirit ✚ by that which achieved the
Law in its entirety. ✚ That which is ✚ was ✚ and will always be.
✚ Omnipotent Agios ✚ Athanatos ✚ Sother ✚ Tetragrammaton ✚
Jehova ✚ Alpha and Omega ✚ the Beginning and the End, through
which all infernal power is extinguished and from which it flees; by
making over this creature, N, the sign of the Cross, on which Jesus
Christ died, and by the invocation of the holy Angels, Archangels,
patriarchs, prophets, apostles, martyrs, confessors, virgins, and of
the Blessed Virgin Mary, and all the saints who have enjoyed the
presence of God since the creation of the world, as well as all the holy
hearts who live in a holy manner within the Church of God. Thus
be gone; and as the fumes of the heart and liver of this fish, which
was burned according to the counsel of the Archangel Raphael, put
to flight the unclean spirit by which Sara was tormented,[3] in the
same way may these blessings drive you out, that you do not dare to
approach this creature, marked by the sign of the holy Cross, within
the space of a hundred thousand steps. Because the command I give
you now is not mine, but from He who was sent from the bosom
of Our Heavenly Father, in order to annihilate your works, as he
destroyed them on the tree of the Cross, and gave us the power to
command you for the glory and use of the faithful, and thus we
command and govern you: Dare not approach by Our Lord Jesus
Christ. Here is the Cross of the Lord, flee, enemies! the Lion of Judah
has prevailed, the Root of David, Alleluia, Amen, Amen, Fiat, Fiat.

HERE ARE THE SEVEN ORISONS
WHICH ONE MUST SAY DURING THE WEEK

By that which you ever bring forth, Lord ✠ sanctify them to you ✠ vivify and bless. ✠ He is by Himself ✠ with Himself ✠ and in Himself, to you, God the Almighty Father, all Honour, Glory, Strength, and Power belong in this century and all other centuries. Amen. We pray, being instructed by the commandment of the Lord, and being led by the Divine Institution, we dare to say:

For Sunday

Our Father, who art in Heaven, Hallowed be Thy Name. Thy Kingdom come, Thy Will be done on Earth, as it is in Heaven. Give us, this day, our daily bread, and forgive us our trespasses, as we forgive those who trespass against us. Lead us not into temptation, but deliver us from evil, for Thine is the Kingdom, the Power, and the Glory. Forever and ever. Amen.

Deliver me, I beseech thee O Lord, your servant N, from all evil, now and to come, of soul and body; and by the intercession of the blessed and forever glorious Virgin Mary, mother of God, and your blessed Apostles Saint Peter, Saint Paul and Saint Andrew, with all your Saints, propitiously grant me peace and sanctity through all the days of my life, that in being so helped by the succour of your mercy I may always be free of the slavery of sin and of all fear of disorder. By the same Jesus Christ your Son, Our Lord, who being God, lives and reigns with you in unity with the Holy Spirit, now and forever. Amen. May the peace of the Lord always be with me. Amen. May the heavenly peace, Lord, that you left to your Disciples, abide resolutely forever in my heart, and be always between me and my enemies, visible and invisible. Amen. May the peace of our Lord Jesus Christ, His face, His body, and His blood, come to my aid, I, N, sinner that I am, serving me as a beneficial protection and defense, and as a consolation to my soul and my body. Amen. Lamb of God, who deigned to be born of the Virgin Mary, and to bear on the tree of the Cross the sins of the world, have pity on my body and my soul. Christ, Lamb of God, through whom all the faithful are saved, give me, in this time and the time to come, eternal peace. Amen.

For Monday

O Lord! O Saviour by whom all things are delivered, deliver me from all evil. O Lord! O Saviour who grants consolation to all beings, grant unto me also, in my necessities, my sufferings, my enterprises and my dangers, and from all kinds of adversities, and from all the traps of my enemies, seen and unseen, deliver me, in the name of the Father who has created all ✠ in the name of the Son, who redeems all ✠ in the name of the Holy Spirit which fulfilled the Law, I commend myself entirely to you. Amen. May the blessing of the Almighty God, the Father, the Son, and the Holy Spirit, always be with me. Amen. ✠ May the blessing of God the Father, who from a single Word made all things, always be with me. ✠ May the blessing of Our Lord, Jesus Christ, Son of the great living God, always be with me. ✠ Amen. May the blessing of the Holy Spirit with its Seven

Gifts always be with me. ✠ *Amen. May the blessing of the Virgin Mary, with her Son, be with me always. Amen. May the blessing and consecration of the bread and wine, that Our Lord, Jesus Christ, made when He offered them to His disciples, saying:*

For Tuesday

Take this and eat: for this is my body, which will be given for you, in memory of me. Amen. ✠ *May the blessings of the holy Angels and Archangels, of the Virtues, the Powers, the Thrones, the Dominations, the Cherubim, the Seraphim, always be with me.* ✠ *Amen. May the blessings of the patriarchs and prophets, the apostles, martyrs, confessors, virgins, and all the saints of God always be with me.* ✠ *Amen. May the blessings of all the Heavens of God always be with me.* ✠ *Amen. May the divine majesty of the Almighty God protect me; may His eternal benefaction lead me; may His inextinguishable benevolence inflame me; may His immense bounty draw me. May the power of the Father preserve me; may the wisdom of the Son vivify me; may the virtue of the Holy Spirit always be between me and all my enemies, seen and unseen. Amen. Power of the Father, strengthen me. Wisdom of the Son, release me. Consolation of the Holy Spirit, comfort me. The Father is Peace, the Son is Life, the Holy Spirit is the remedy of Consolation and Salvation. Amen. May the divinity of God bless me; may His humanity strengthen me. Amen. May his piety stir me. Amen. May His Love preserve me. Amen. O Jesus Christ, Son of the great living God, have pity on this poor sinner.*

For Wednesday

O Emmanuel! defend me from the evil spirit and from all my enemies, visible and invisible and deliver me from all evil. Christ the King came in peace; God made man and suffered mercifully for us; may Jesus Christ, king of peace, be always between my enemies and I. Amen. Christ is victorious. ✠ Christ reigns. ✠ Christ commands. ✠ May Christ defend me always from all evil. Amen. May Jesus Christ deign to order that I be victorious over all my enemies. Amen. Here is the Cross of Our Lord Jesus Christ: flee, my enemies. The Lion of the tribe of Judah has prevailed, the Root of David: Alleluia Alleluia Alleluia. Saviour of the world, save me and help me, you, who redeemed me by your Cross and your most precious blood; help me, I entreat you, O God. O Agios ✠ O theos ✠ Agios Ischyros ✠ Agios Athanatos ✠ Eleison Himas. Holy God, strong God, merciful and immortal God, take pity on me, your servant, N. Be my support, Lord, do not abandon me; do not look upon me in contempt, God my redeemer, but forever come to my aid, Lord God my Saviour.

For Thursday

Fill my eyes with light, Lord, so that I never sleep in Death, and may my enemy not say that he is stronger than me. May the Lord be with me, and I will not fear that which man can do against me. O gentle Jesus, preserve me, help me, save me: in the name of Jesus let all in Heaven, on Earth and in Hell genuflect, and every tongue confess that our Lord Jesus Christ enjoys the glory of His Father. Amen. I know without doubt, O Jesus, that in the day and hour in which I invoke you I will be saved. O merciful Lord Jesus Christ, only Son of the living God, who through the virtue of your most precious name has made so many miracles, and who has given a remedy so profuse, to us who had such great need for it, for by the virtue of your name the demons take flight, the blind see, the deaf hear, the lame walk, the dumb speak, the lepers are healed, the sick obtain their health, and the dead are brought back to life. For when the name of your very gentle Son, Jesus, is spoken, one hears a sweet melody in the ear, honey is felt in the mouth, the demon is put to flight, all kneel, the celestial spirits rejoice, evil temptations are eradicated, all infirmities are healed; one gains many indulgences; the struggles which are between the world, the devil and the flesh are eliminated, and many other benefits will follow them, for whosoever will call upon the name of God will be saved, that name which was called by the Angel before he was conceived in the womb of the Blessed Virgin.

For Friday

O gentle name, name strengthening the heart of man, name of life, salvation and joy; precious name, joyous, glorious, and filled with Grace, name fortifying sinners, name which redeems us, ruling and governing all the motions of the universe. May it please you, O most pious Jesus! that by the same most precious virtue of your name to deign to make the demons flee from me; enlighten me, O Lord, I who am blind; cause me to hear, I who am deaf; guide my steps, I who am lame; return to me Thy Word, I who am dumb; heal my

leprosy, give to me health again, I who am sick. Awaken me from
Death, and surround me entirely, within and without, so that being
provided with your most sacred Name, I may live always in you, in
praise and honour of you, you who are praiseworthy; for you are
the most glorious Lord and the eternal Lord, and the eternal Son
of God, in whom and by whom all things rejoice and are governed.
Praise, honour and glory to you, now and forever. Amen. May Jesus
always be in my heart, may Jesus be always on my lips may Jesus
be always in my depths. Amen. May God my Lord, Jesus Christ, be
always within me to restore me; may He surround me to lead me;
may He be after me to preserve me, before me to maintain me,
upon me to bless me; may He be between me to enliven me, with me
to rule over me, above me to strengthen me; may He always be with
me to remove all the suffering of an eternal death, He who, with the
Father and the Holy Spirit, lives and reigns now and forever. Amen.

For Saturday

May Jesus, Son of Mary, Lord and Redeemer of the world, be propitious and merciful with me, may He grant me a sound and submissive mind, to return honor and respect to Him, and may He grant
us deliverance from our ills in the place where we are: and no-one
has laid a hand on Him for His hour is not yet come, the one who
is, was and will be forever, Alpha and Omega, God and man, the
beginning and the end; may this invocation be an eternal protection
for me, in the name of Jesus of Nazareth, king of the Jews, mark
of victory, son of the Virgin Mary, have pity on this poor sinner, N,

and lead me, according to your mercy, on the way of eternal salvation. Amen. Yet Jesus, knowing all that must come to pass, came forward and asked, "Whom do you seek?" They responded, "Jesus of Nazareth." And Jesus said to them, "I am he." Yet Judas, who had betrayed him, was also present amongst them. So when Jesus had said to them: I am he, they all fell back, dropping to the ground. Jesus asked them, once again, "Whom do you seek?" They said to him, "Jesus of Nazareth." Jesus replied, "I already told you, I am he. If it is me that you seek, let these men go." May Jesus, sacrificed for me, expiating my crime by His Cross, make me pleasant to His eyes, and may at last my purged soul, being separated from my body, reign with Him in heaven. Amen. Jesus is the way. ✛ Jesus is the life. ✛ Jesus is the truth. ✛ Jesus suffered. ✛ Jesus was crucified. ✛ Jesus Christ, Son of the living God, have mercy on me. ✛ Yet Jesus, passing in the midst of them, stood, and none laid a hand on Him, for His hour had not yet come.

The Pentagram[4]

MYSTERIOUS ORISON

I implore you all, Saints, Martyrs, Confessors, and Virgins of God, to intercede with Our Lord Jesus Christ — who lives and reigns in eternity with the Holy Spirit — for the sake of this poor sinner, so that I may enjoy His holy Paradise. Amen.

May the God of Abraham ✠ the God of Isaac ✠ the God of Jacob ✠ of Aaron ✠ of Ely ✠ the God of Noah; ✠ lastly, may God be with me always. Amen. Blessed Archangels Michael, Raphael, Gabriel, Cherubim and Seraphim, all the holy Angels and holy Archangels, and all the other Saints, may you come to my aid all the days of my eternal life. Amen. Amedan ✠ Austos ✠ Taustazo ✠ Barachedio ✠ Memor ✠ Gedita ✠ Eleison ✠ Maton ✠ Igion ✠ Frigam ✠ Fides ✠ Valey ✠ Unis ✠ Regnat ✠ Sadau ✠ Hagios ✠ O Theos ✠ Sanctus Deus ✠ Hagios ✠ Athanatos ✠ Eleison Himas ✠ Holy Immortal, have pity on this poor sinner. Amen.

Blessed Angels Michael ✠ Raphael ✠ Uriel ✠ Gabriel ✠ Barachiel ✠ Cherubim ✠ and Seraphim ✠ intercede for me near to God; here, ✠ the cross of Our Lord Jesus Christ. Hence, flee, my enemies, the Lion of the tribe of Judah has prevailed: the Root of David, Alleluia. Deliver me, my God, from my enemies and out of the hands of those who commit evil, and those who would soak their hands in my blood, Amen. O God, let the glory of your Name shine forth, and save me, make manifest your power, in sustaining the goodness of my cause. ✠ You who saves Kings, who redeemed David your servant, deliver me from the sword of my enemies, who maliciously seek to destroy me. Jesus Christ conquers ✠ Jesus reigns ✠ Jesus Christ commands ✠ May Jesus Christ preserve and defend me from all evil. Amen.

ORISON AGAINST THE ADVERSITIES OF THE WORLD

He will break the bow, he will shatter the weapons, and will throw the shields in the fire. They abide in peace, He says, and they acknowledge my power and my Divinity; My Glory will burst forth in all nations and I will be exalted on the Earth. Amen.

TO THE VIRGIN

Make us feel that you are our Mother, in commending our prayers to Him who desired to become your Son to redeem us.

A VERY EFFECTIVE ORISON

The righteousness of the Lord has made manifest all His power, the righteousness of the Lord has shown His power in raising me, the righteousness of the Lord has demonstrated that such is His power; life will not be taken from me, on the contrary, I will live and I will tell of the wonders of the Lord. The Lord has punished me by His justice, and chastised me on account of my crime, but His compassion has delivered me from death. Amen.

When my enemies drew near to destroy me and threw themselves on me as savage beasts which throw themselves on their prey to devour it. At the same time as they made their persecution felt, God impressed on them their weakness and they succumbed to the traps they had set for me.

ORISON OF GREAT VIRTUE

O Theos, O God, make the Glory of your Name shine forth and save me! Agios, as soon as I confessed my crime to you and no longer concealed my offences. Holy. Holy. Holy. Open my mind and teach me to adore, glorify, and exalt you. O Theos, Eleison Himas: may those who offend me feel the effect of your justice, almighty Lord: Lord, crush those who advance to attack me: Messias, Soter, Emmanuel, take up your weapons and your shield and save me. Jesus, arise and come to my aid; bread, flower, light, spear, esprit, door, stone, rock, Athanatos, undying God, draw your sword in my favour; Ischyros, mighty God, decide the downfall of those who persecute me; Jesus my Savior, prevent them from defending themselves, sustain my soul and assure me of your desire to save it; True Panton, Panstraton, Craton, Sabaoth, Lord of Hosts, do not abandon me to the fury of my enemies and save me from those who rise from every direction in their plan to vanquish me; My Lord, allow yourself to yield to my prayers, come and deliver me from those who afflict me and slander me. O my God, witness my anguish and the evils I rightly suffer for my sins; deign to cleanse me of my sins; hasten, and purify me by your grace so that the spirit of fornication be utterly destroyed in me, inflame me to do all manner of good works constantly, and grant me the strength and virtue of the Father, the Son and the Holy Spirit who reign eternally and without end through all time. Amen.

After this, it is necessary to say a *Pater* and an *Ave*.

ORISON

Pitiful and merciful Lord, in whom is infinite compassion and patience; O great and terrible God, I make a sincere confession of my faults, I open and reveal my wounds to you; I beseech you in your ineffable compassion to forget my sins and the woes I have committed against you, since you yourself meant that you do not desire the death of the sinner, but rather that he transforms himself and lives. Amen. I confess, I have sinned, even in your presence I sinned: my life is but a web of sins and troubles; in a word, my soul is smothered and extinguished by a plague of iniquities: learning, pride, sloth, avarice, luxury, wrath, impatience, wickedness, envy, gluttony, intoxication, lust, rapaciousness, theft, perjury, foolish words, insolence, ignorance, negligence and an infinity of sins that have brought death to my soul: my heart is corrupted and poisoned, as are my speech, my sight, my hearing, my smell and my touch, in all ways, in word, thought and deed; withal, I dread nothing whilst I have the pleasure of being in your divine presence. I beg you most urgently, O my God, whose compassion is without bounds, deliver me from my pitiful weaknesses and forgive me in the same way that you forgave the sinful woman: Lord, allow me to give you the kiss of peace, as you have permitted her to ceaselessly kiss your sacred feet, to bathe them with her tears and dry them with her hair. Grant me also a vast love for you, as the number of my sins against your divine Majesty has been great, that by your infinite mercy you will forgive me all; deign to grant me pardon also for my old faults and the grace not to commit them in the future; give me also the grace to receive your divine mercy absolutely before I die, do not allow me to end my days without having been granted absolution from my sins. But as I am a poor sinner and you have the compassion to forgive me, I will praise and give thanks to you for eternity, O my God, who in your infinite mercy made me in your image and likeness, and stooped (regenerating me in the sacred waters of baptism) to embrace me and place me amongst your beloved children. Once more I give you everlasting praise and thanks for having preserved my life from childhood until the present; you still have the compassion to await the truth, that by your infinite mercy I return to repentance and forsake this multitude of sins that I have committed against your divine majesty: my language is too poor, O my God, to give the praises and glory that are due unto you for such a salient blessing, which through your excessive mercy, has so often saved me from the constant vicissitudes, predicaments, calamities and woes in which I have found myself, and has until this moment preserved me from eternal torments as much as from the torments of the flesh. I reiterate my most humble thanks, praise and glory to you, who by your pure Bounty, desired to grant me health of my body, tranquility in my life, and finally, good actions and charity; in a word, if I possess them, I am beholden to your endless mercy. Grant me, if it pleases you O my God, the inestimable gift of your mildness, and strengthen in me the good that you have had the generosity to bestow upon me, banish from me all that causes you displeasure. Cleanse me and deliver me from my tribulations, and from all the evils which surround me; may it please you to rule my thoughts, words and actions according to your holy Will, and make me joyful and happy always, even in the midst of my adversities, and conform my desires at all times to your holy Will, you who live and reign in eternity. Amen.

AGAINST HUMAN FRAILTY

Holy ✠ strong ✠ immortal and merciful God ✠ my Saviour, do not allow us to be exposed to a cruel and distressing death; ✠ remember us, who belong to you in eternity.

ORISON

O God, knowing that we are exposed to so many perils and dangers, that we could not survive by reason of our human frailty, may it please you to grant us salvation of body and soul. Deliver us from dangers with your help, we whom you rightly punish on account of our sins; we entreat you, by Our Lord Jesus Christ. Amen.

ORISON AGAINST ENEMIES

Yet Jesus passing in the midst of them, went on His way: May the Lord be blessed from day to day, and as He is Our Savior, He will lead us fortunately on the way He has marked for us. ✠ Now, Jesus, may the darkness blind them, having no use of their eyes, and that, for the mark of their indignity, they are always bent to the ground. ✠ Now, Jesus, pour upon them the effects of your indignation, so your righteous anger gives them continual alarm. ✠ May the horror and the terror destroy their courage, by the idea of your strength alone. Lord, make them motionless as stones, until I, N, who am your creature, redeemed by your precious blood, have passed by. ✠

Lord, the strength of your arm is marvelously demonstrated; it will exterminate a powerful enemy by its strength, abasing the pride of the impious who rise against me. ✠ Deliver me, Lord Jesus, keep me from those who rise against me on all sides in their intent to destroy me. ✠ Lord Jesus, deliver me from the hands of these evil-doers and wrest me from those of the unjust. ✠ Deliver me, Jesus, from the hands of those who commit evil; save me and defend me from those who seek to spill my blood. ✠ Glory be to the Father; to the Son; and to the Holy Spirit, today and always, in this century and for all centuries, from the beginning and for all eternity. Amen.

Archangel Saint Michael

ORISON

O Lord Jesus Christ, Son of the great living God who, at the hour of your most sacred Passion, said to those who were seeking you, Whom do you seek? Upon hearing those words they drew back and fell to the ground. Deign, I beg you, to deliver me, in the same way, from my enemies and their wicked intentions, saying to them: let N pass unharmed, for he is my creature; and they can do me no evil, at any time, neither now nor in the future. You, who lives and reigns with God the Father, in unity with the Holy Spirit. Amen.

VERY USEFUL ORISON FOR THOSE WHO TRAVEL

Agla ✠ Pentagrammaton ✠ On ✠ Athanatos ✠ Anasareon ✠ On ✠ Pentareon ✠ Door ✠ Cross ✠ Agratam ✠ Flock ✠ Light ✠ Teta tustus ✠ of man ✠ Tomon ✠ Tetragrammaton ✠ Jesus ✠ God ✠ Lord of all thimgs ✠ merciful ✠ most high ✠ my Lord, deliver me, N, who am your creature, deliver me I say, by all these holy Names, remember me, whose recourse is to you, my God who is everywhere. Lord, in your Bounty, deliver me from the traps of my enemies, visible as well as invisible. I ask you, Lord, by the strength and virtue of this holy Cross, ✠ by the merits of all your saints. Yet Jesus passing in the midst of them, went on His way. ✠ Jesus Christ, Son of the great living God, ✠ have pity on me.

ADMIRABLE ORISON TO THE CROSS OF THE SAVIOR

✠ *Cross of Jesus Christ, save me.* ✠ *Cross of Jesus Christ, defend me.* ✠ *Cross of Jesus Christ, preserve me from all evil,* ✠ *may those who offend me feel the effect of your justice.* ✠ *Almighty God, annihilate those who draw near to attack me.* ✠ *Messiah,* ✠ *Lord of Hosts* ✠ *Sother* ✠ *Emmanuel, pick up your weapons and take your shield. Lord of Hosts, Our Lord Jesus Christ, pull me from the mire so I shall not perish.* ✠ *Holy God, deliver me from the hatred of my enemies.* ✠ *Eli, deliver me from the depths of the waters which surround me.* ✠ *O my Salvation, do not let me descend into the abyss of the sea.* ✠ *O Athanatos, may I not feel the ferocity of the fire.* ✠ *O my Refuge, do not let the contagion of the infernal pit pollute my mouth or sense of smell,* ✠ *but you, my Liberator, open my mouth and exterminate my enemies.* ✠ *O Athanatos, tell my soul that you wish to save it.* ✠ *Tetragrammaton, do not abandon me to the fury of my enemies.* ✠ *Adonay, keep me from those who rise against me from all quarters in their plan to slay me.* ✠ *Jesus, Savior of the world, save me,* ✠ *bread of life, immutable flower,* ✠ *strength and door of Paradise.* ✠ *May the blessing of the Blessed Virgin Mary and her Son be always upon me,* ✠ *may the blessing of Our Lord Jesus Christ and the holy Apostles be upon me,* ✠ *may the blessing of the Holy Spirit be upon me,* ✠ *may the blessing of God the Almighty Father, be upon me, with His holy angels and His saints.* ✠ *May the blessing of the Holy Trinity, the Father, the Son, and the Holy Spirit be upon me.* ✠ *May the blessing of Saint Catherine of Mount Sinaï be upon me,* ✠ *may the blessing of all the holy angels, archangels, patriarchs, prophets, apostles, evangelists, martyrs, all the virgins, monks and pontiffs be upon me.*

ORISON OF THE BLESSED VIRGIN

I greet you, glorious Virgin, Star more brilliant than the Sun, redder than the new Rose, whiter than the lily, more elevated in Heaven than any saint, you are revered by all the Earth. Accept my homage and help me through your divine assistance. Amen.

Say the *Pater* and *Ave* in their entirety.

EXHORTATION TO JESUS CHRIST

Hagios, invisible Lord, I humbly beg you to deliver me from death. I entreat you by your Name; Oston, condescend to help me, a poor sinner whose sole refuge is in you, ✠ Tetragrammaton, you are the King of kings, God the Father, Lord of lords, and it is in you alone that I place my faith, you who govern and reign over all things in Heaven and on Earth. I entreat you, have compassion and take pity on this poor sinner, I, N, beg you once more, deliver me from all my enemies, Lord, may Geban, Suth, and Sutan also have pity on me, in the name of the Father ✠ and of the Son, ✠ and of the Holy Spirit. Amen. The first name of God is Oston, the second Orthon. And when God said, Let there be light, it was at once: the third name is Lophias, ✠ in the Name of the Lord and the indivisible Trinity, ✠ Antariton ✠ Ituriensis ✠ Adonay, save me, Chedes and Ei, and O Theos Adonay. Amen.

DELIVER ME, LORD, BY THE SIGN OF THE TAU CROSS

In the name of the Father, and of the Son, and of the Holy Spirit. Amen. In the name of the most holy and indivisible Trinity. Amen. ✠ I conjure you, all kinds of weapons there may be, knives, swords, arrows, double-edged tools, lances, nails, and all other metal weapons, by the Father, the Son, and the Holy Spirit, that you cannot wound me, N, at all, nor shed my blood, and until I expressly order you thrice, they cannot draw my blood while I hold them in my hand: Yet, if the weapons of my adversaries enable them to wound me, I beg you urgently to melt them as wax by your Virtue. ✠ I entreat you once more, whatsoever weapons you may be, by the iron spear wielded by the soldier Longinus to open the side of Our Lord Jesus Christ, from whence he shed blood and water, to be able neither to wound nor harm me, nor to spill my blood. N. ✠ I entreat you once more, by the pillar to which Our Lord Jesus Christ was bound and lead before the Judge, not to wound me nor shed my blood. ✠ I entreat you once more, by the three nails which pierced the hands and feet of Our Lord Jesus Christ, not to wound me nor

mark me with any blood. ✣ I entreat you once more, whatsoever weapons you may be, by the iron grill on which the martyr Saint Lawrence was burned, neither to harm, wound nor spill my blood. ✣ I entreat you again, whatsoever kinds of weapons you may be, by the sword with which Saint Paul was decapitated, neither to wound me, nor to shed my blood. ✣ I entreat you again, whatsoever kinds of weapons you may be, by the iron bands in which Saint Agnes was held and tortured for two years, that you cannot wound me nor shed my blood. ✣ I entreat you one again, all weapons, by the iron instrument upon which blessed Saint Agatha was hung, neither to wound me nor shed my blood. ✣ I entreat you once more, all weapons, swords, knives, double-edged tools, and all kinds of weapons, by the seventy two Names of God known to us, and by the immutable God who governs the Heavens and the Earth, and all things contained therein, to glorify Him eternally. ✣ I entreat you also by the holy Name of God, Fimandolum, by the strength with which Joshua vanquished twelve kings. ✣ I entreat you also, by the holy Name of God, Tetragrammaton. ✣ Jot ✣ Set ✣ Neor ✣ Nain ✣ He. ✣ I entreat you by all the joys and sufferings of the blessed Mary, perpetual Virgin, ✣ I also entreat you by all the apostles, evangelists, martyrs and by the twenty four elders, by all the doctors, confessors, monks, and hermits, by all the virgins and widows, by all the saints of God, by the most holy pledge of Our Lord Jesus Christ, by His true and sacred words, by which none have the power or authority to injure, nor wound, nor shed blood ✣ for I myself, passing in the midst of them, will say: here ✣ is the Cross of the Lord; therefore vanish, my enemies, and take flight, the Lion of the tribe of Judah has prevailed, the Root of David. ✣ Deliver us, Lord, from your enemies, by the virtue of the sign of the cross. ✠ Precious cross, I entreat you to receive me, and to preserve me from my enemies by the virtue of He who was nailed to you. ✠ Spirit of wisdom and understanding, ✠ spirit of counsel and of strength, ✠ spirit of science ✠ and of piety, ✠ spirit of awe for Our Lord, defend me and protect me from all arms, and even from their injuries, from the wounds made by swords, spears, bolts, arrows, and from harm from all weapons, whatsoever they may be, I entreat you to protect your creature N from them, ✠ save me, ✠ bless me, ✠ sanctify me ✠ and safeguard me from all wounds, by the sign ✠ of your holy Cross. ✠ I entreat you by your five wounds, ✠ Hely ✠ Eloy ✠ Het ✠ Clavis ✠ Egon ✠ Eth ✠ Huc ✠ Proth ✠ Ceretas ✠ A ✠ Feros ✠ Homo ✠ the King of Glory comes in peace, ✠ the Word was made flesh, (and lives amongst us: and we saw the glory of God as the only Son of the Father), He was full of grace and truth.

ORISON TO MAKE A WOMAN FAITHFUL
Adonay Job. Magister dixît.

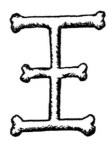

O good Jesus! hear me, Emmanuel, Emmanuel, Sathor, adorable Yeśhua Tetragrammaton, Heli, Heli, Heli, Læbe, Hey, Hamy, this is my body, Tetragrammaton, come to my aid now and always. ✠ *Jesus is victorious,* ✠ *Jesus reigns,* ✠ *Jesus commands,* ✠ *may Jesus Christ preserve me from all evil and lead me eternally to good fortune. Amen. You will not do unto him any injury, and nor śhall the arrows fired by day, nor the ambuśhes prepared during darkness, nor the attacks of the Demon who opposes at noon, nor the legions of warriors whiċh fall around you, and the ten thousand at your right, yet none will draw close to you, and thus may my enemies be confounded, but do not allow, Lord, for this to befall me: let them be consumed by fear, but not me; O my God, make them feel your vengeance, and make them doubly repent.* ✠ *Yet Jesus, passing in the midst of them, went on His way: and me, I will pass in the midst of them, uplifted by the great Name Adonay.* ✠ *Yet Jesus, passing in*

the midst of them, went unseen. My God, I entreat you, let me pass
in the midst of my enemies, this day and while I live, without any
danger to body and soul. ✠ If it is me you seek, then let these men
go; ✠ as Our Lord Jesus Christ spoke these words with his own lips,
may he also stoop to keep me and protect me from my enemies. ✠
Forbid them, Lord, from doing unto me any injury, nor let them do
any evil. Thus flee, my enemies, and be gone, ✠ in the name of the
Father, ✠ of the Son, ✠ and of the Holy Spirit, ✠ Alpha and Omega,
have pity on me, close the hearts and mouths of my enemies, so that
neither man nor woman, nor any treacherous or poisoned tongue,
shall be over me, nor that I suffer any sign of it. O God, save me,
your servant N, who hopes in you and honours your Name, deliver
me from all peril and danger. Amen. ✠ ✠ ✠ ✠ ✠ May the horror
and terror cut down their courage, only by the idea of your strength.
Lord, make them motionless as stones, until your creature, of whom
you are master and protector, has passed. ✠ Lord, I commend my
spirit into your hands, ✠ If it is me you seek, then let those men
go. ✠ ✠ ✠ But you, Lord, use sorrows and afflictions as a bit and
a bridle, to bring back to you those who behave as beasts, straying
far from you. Saint Michael, Saint Gabriel, Saint Raphael, defend
me and sustain me in the struggle that I must uphold against my
enemies, and deliver me from all peril. Amen. Deliver me, my God,
from my enemies, seen and unseen; do not abandon me, Lord, I who
am your creature. Holy and Blessed Virgin Mary, deliver me from
the snares of my enemies. I greet you, Mary, full of grace, ✠ my Lord
Jesus Christ, who delivered the apostle, Saint Peter, from prison, and
Saint Paul of Damascus, Saint John the Evangelist from boiling oil,
also deign, Lord, to deliver and keep me from captivity. Holy and

Blessed Virgin Mary, deliver me from torments and from prison, by your virginal heart, pure and without blemish, and by your holy salvation, may your creature N be blessed and delivered from all peril and captivity. ✠ Agla ✠ Lacta ✠ Sancta et El ✠ Ischyros ✠ Heloy ✠ Ceophobus ✠ Sabaoth ✠ Heleyon ✠ Ja ✠ Tetragrammaton ✠ Ely ✠ Adonay ✠ Sadai ✠ Fiat ✠ Fiat ✠ Fiat, may their eyes be blinded by the darkness and, as a mark of their indignity, always be bent to the earth. When you see me weighed down by the excess of afflictions, and at risk of losing my life, I will not fear these dangers, Lord, because you are there and will deliver me from them, and take my part. If it is me that you seek, then let those men go. Receive me favorably, Lord, and confound my enemies, for you are my shield and my consolation. Honour be to God the Father, who in His Bounty desires to deliver me; ✠ and I put all my consolation in the hope of your help and protection; ✠ and in Jesus Christ by His divine mercy. ✠ May the peace of Our Lord Jesus Christ be always with me, with the veneration He has for His Father. Amen. ✠ For this is my body, ✠✠ that they adore. Amen. ✠ Behold the cross of the Lord, disappear and flee, demons and malign spirits, my enemies: the Lion of the tribe of Judah has prevailed, the Root of David. Alleluia. Alleluia. Alleluia. Deliver me, my God, by this sign of the cross, ✠ from my enemies and all evil. ✠ Cross of Jesus Christ, help me, ✠ cross of Jesus Christ, rescue me, ✠ cross of Jesus Christ, save me, ✠ cross of Jesus Christ, defend me against all my enemies and from every peril and danger. Hagios ✠ O Theos ✠ Hagios ✠ Ischyros ✠ Ragios ✠ Athanatos ✠ Eleison ✠ Himas ✠✠ Jesus of Nazareth, King of the Jews, let the Glory of your Name burst forth. Amen.

ETERNAL PRAISE TO GOD

*My enemies, I present myself to you, endowed with the grace of
God, His Love, with the humility of Jesus Christ who is God, with the
strength and the Word of the Holy Spirit who is also God, with the
glorious standard of the cross, accompanied by the glorious Virgin
Mary, the purity of Abel, the help of Noah, the faith of Abraham, the
obedience of Isaac, the innocence of Jacob, the patience of Job, the
gentleness of Moses, the holiness of Aaron, the wisdom of Solomon,
the victory of Joshua, the justice of David, the strength of Samson,
the power of Peter, the chastity of John, the word of Matthew, the
contrition of Gregory, the prayer of Clement, the splendor of the
Moon, the light of the Sun, and the latitude of the Heavens, the
longitude of the Earth, the depth of the Sea, the course of the River
Jordan, the glory of holy Jerusalem, with the help of all the Saints,
and that of Our Lord Jesus Christ by whom all things were made:
may this same Son of God, who was born of the blessed Virgin Mary,
illuminate my spirit in the light of His Glory and change the hostility
of my enemies into love; may their bad will, wicked intentions and
pernicious plans be annihilated by His gentleness, and by virtue of
all the Saints' names, of which we have spoken above, and by that
of the Almighty God, may all the efforts of my enemies come to
naught: and may this same God born of the blessed Virgin Mary,
transform all your evil and diabolical thoughts into good, to my
benefit. Amen. Amen. Amen. May the true God Jesus Christ, full of
tenderness and compassion for mankind, of whom He is the Judge
of the living and dead; may the holy Names of the Almighty God be
a powerful shield and helmet against the venomous features of my*

enemies, so they cannot harm me, N, who am God's creature; may they be rendered fusible at my approach, as wax melts in the heat of fire. Amen. ✠ Jesus Christ is victorious, ✠ Jesus Christ reigns, ✠ Jesus Christ commands, ✠ may Jesus Christ deliver and preserve me from all adversity and keep me even from death, for I am His creature. Amen. ✠ Jesus Christ is King, He comes in peace, and God made man. Yet Jesus, passing in the midst of them, went on His way. ✠ All is consumed: ✠ Who do you seek ✠ It is I ✠ If it is I whom you seek, let these other men go. ✠ Yet Jesus, passing in the midst of them, went on His way. ✠ All is consumed: ✠ and lowering His head, He surrendered His spirit. Praise be to God, and to the blessed Virgin Mary, who will destroy you, ✠ who will remove you, ✠ who will tear you from your dwelling-places, He will uproot you from the earth of the living to admonish your spite. In the name of the Father, ✠ and of the Son, ✠ and of the Holy Spirit, ✠ Amen.

May all beings, heavenly, terrestrial and infernal, genuflect at the name of Jesus alone, and may every tongue attest that Our Lord Jesus Christ sits at the right hand of God the Father exulting in His Glory. Thus, we must glorify the cross of Our Lord Jesus Christ, in which is found our salvation, our life, our spiritual resurrection, and by which Jesus Christ redeemed us. May God pour on us the almighty effects of His bounty, and may it fill us with His blessings; may the light of His face shine upon us, and may He help us by His mercy.

THE PRESENT FIGURE, FORTY TIMES IN LENGTH,
GIVES THE HEIGHT OF JESUS CHRIST

This was found in Constantinople enclosed in a gold cross; whosoever wears ît upon themselves can have no better protećtion, and will not to suffer a sudden death, neîther by fire nor by water, not by arrows nor by storms; neîther by thunder nor by venom; not from evil ſpirîts, neîther by false judgments nor false wîtness. Moreover, if a pregnant woman wears this, invoking the grace of Our Lord Jesus Christ, ſhe will not have pain or danger in ćhildbirth.

EXEMPLAR OF THE LETTER FROM ABGAR, KING OF EDESSA, *written to Jesus Christ in Jerusalem, and sent by the courier Ananas.*

Abgar, son of Theopathos, King of Edessa, to Jesus our Saviour, who showed himself in Jerusalem: greetings.

I heard talk here of your renown, and the great wonders you perform, and the healings you make without the aid of medicines and beneficial herbs, that your word alone is enough to return sight to the blind, make the lame to walk again, cleanse lepers and drive out unclean spirits, you return health to those who are far from you, and you even resurrect the dead. Word of such actions has persuaded me to believe that either you are a God descended from Heaven, or that you are the Son of God — to do such great things — and has prompted me to write to you, to kindly request you to come to my country and return to me the health that a long illness has deprived me of.

I learned that the Jews are angry with you and set snares for you; come to me, my city is quite minor, yet well-provided for and strong enough to protect you.

I greet you and commend myself to you.

THE WORDS WHICH SHOULD BE SAID BEFORE MAKING THE PENTACLE WHICH IS SHOWN IN THE FIGURE.

Lord, give me strength against my enemies, hear my prayer, and may my cries reach unto you.

The words which are in the circle mean in English: *In this sign you will conquer.* You must now exorcise and perfume the Pentacle, then write the following Orison:

THE ANSWER OF JESUS CHRIST,
with an Orison of admirable virtues.

You are blessed, King Abgar, to have believed in me, albeit without having seen me, for many have seen and yet did not believe in me. As for what you wrote regarding my coming to you, it is necessary that I first accomplish here all the things for which I was sent: after I have completed them, I will send one of my disciples to you, named Thaddeus, so he can heal your illness, and give life to you, and all those around you. This is why I send you this letter, written in my own hand, so that wherever you might be, whether at home or at sea, on a river, or in combat against Pagans, or Christians, or in any place wheresoever, your enemies and adversaries will have no dominion over you, and you will have nothing to fear from the traps of the Demon. Impure spirits, lightning and thunder will be unable to harm you if you carry this prayer devoutly with you. I love you, O Abgar, and I promise you my salvation, may my peace be always with you.

Abgar, having received and read this letter, exclaimed with tears in his eyes: *O Jesus Christ, Son of the living God, Almighty God, full of mercy, be favorable to me in all things, in the Name of the most holy and indivisible Trinity, the Father, the Son and the Holy Spirit. I entreat you, all weapons, by the Father, the Son and the Holy Spirit; I entreat you, sticks, knives, spears, swords, daggers, arrows, clubs, garottes, and all other kinds of weapons, by the seventy two Names of God, by His infinite virtue, and His supreme power; I entreat you by the spear with which the soldier Longinus pierced the side of Jesus, from whence He shed blood and water, by the other sacred names of God, ✠ Joth ✠ Hoet ✠ Vari ✠ Hei ✠ do not wound me, NN, a servant of God, and do not spill my blood: I entreat you, weapons of all kinds, by the virtue of the holy Names of God, ✠ Hel ✠ Ya ✠ Hye ✠ Yae ✠ Adonay ✠ Cados ✠ Oborel ✠ Eloym ✠ Agla ✠ Agiel ✠ Azel ✠ Sadon ✠ Esul ✠ Heloy ✠ Heloyn ✠ Delis ✠ Yeui ✠ Yacer ✠ Del ✠ Yosi ✠ Helim ✠ Rasaël ✠ Rasaël ✠ Paliel ✠ Mammiel ✠ Oncha ✠ Dilaton ✠ Xaday ✠ Alma ✠ Pavix ✠*

Alim ✠ *Catival* ✠ *Utauzaraf* ✠ *Zalphi* ✠ *Eala* ✠ *Carsalay* ✠ *Faffua* ✠ *Hictimi* ✠ *Sed* ✠ *Der* ✠ *Agla* ✠ *Aglaia* ✠ *Pamiel et Pannion* ✠ *Oniel* ✠ *On* ✠ *Homon* ✠ *Oreon* ✠ *Lestram* ✠ *Panteon* ✠ *Bamboy* ✠ *Ya* ✠ *Emmanuel* ✠ *Yoth* ✠ *Lucaf* ✠ *On* ✠ *Via* ✠ *Calip* ✠ *Lon* ✠ *Israël* ✠ *Miel* ✠ *Cyel* ✠ *Pycel* ✠ *Patriteron* ✠ *Fafaron* ✠ *Leuyon,* *Yael* ✠ *that you may not wound me, N, who is the servant of God, nor shed my blood: it is said that you will not break the bones of he whom the Lord has made strong. His virtue exalts me; I will not die, but will live and tell of the wonders of the Lord: the Lord has admonished me, and he did not deliver me unto death; praise and thanksgiving be unto Him. Amen.*

THE GREAT HOLY POPE LEO WROTE TO CHARLES,
King of France, saying: *Whosoever carries on themselves these holy Names, no mortal enemy may harm him; and it is necessary to note that contained within is the name of Christ, Agla, which serves to steel yourself against adversities, and which being seen & worn everyday, will preserve you from an unholy death.*

In the Name of the Father ✠ *and of the Son* ✠ *and of the Holy Spirit. Amen. Arise, indivisible Trinity* ✠ *God Messiah* ✠ *Sother* ✠ *Emmanuel* ✠ *Sabaoth* ✠ *Adonay* ✠ *Coteraton* ✠ *Ysion* ✠ *Son* ✠ *Lon* ✠ *Con* ✠ *Son* ✠ *Osiam* ✠ *Salvation* ✠ *Life* ✠ *Truth* ✠ *Ve* ✠ *Wisdom* ✠ *I am* ✠ *what I am* ✠ *I am the Lamb* ✠ *the Ewe* ✠ *the Calf* ✠ *the Serpent* ✠ *the Ram* ✠ *the Lion* ✠ *the Green* ✠ *the Sun* ✠ *Agla* ✠ *the Image* ✠ *the Bread* ✠ *the Life* ✠ *the Flower* ✠ *the Mountain* ✠ *the Door* ✠ *the Fountain* ✠ *the Stone* ✠ *the Rock* ✠ *the Angle* ✠ *the*

Pastor ✠ *the Prophet* ✠ *the Priest* ✠ *the Saint* ✠ *the Immortal* ✠ *the great King* ✠ *I am the first* ✠ *and the second, Lion* ✠ *third, Flower* ✠ *fourth, Follower* ✠ *fifth, Earth* ✠ *sixth, Premax* ✠ *seventh, Sagai* ✠ *eighth, Bethlehem* ✠ *ninth, Tetragrammaton* ✠ *tenth, Seloy* ✠ *eleventh, Eloy* ✠ *Satos* ✠ *Ecaton* ✠ *Himas* ✠ *Eleison* ✠ *Saviour* ✠ *Alpha* ✠ *the First* ✠ *and Omega, the Last* ✠ *the first-born* ✠ *the Beginning* ✠ *the Consoler* ✠ *the Mediator* ✠ *Word* ✠ *Yschyros* ✠ *Glory* ✠ *Light* ✠ *World* ✠ *Cornerstone* ✠ *Saint* ✠ *Immortal* ✠ *Jesus, the Father* ✠ *the Almighty Son* ✠ *merciful Holy Spirit* ✠ *eternal Purity* ✠ *Creator* ✠ *Redeemer* ✠ *Angel of great counsel* ✠ *Trin* ✠ *God* ✠ *Holy, Holy, Holy, the Lord of Lords,* ✠ *the God of Gods* ✠ *ineffable God* ✠ *beyond understanding* ✠ *righteous Judge* ✠ *and always in combat, by Sea or water, Gedebelone, S.E.Q.P., and always on the path to war: King of the Jews, take pity on us: Alleluia.*

O my Lord God most Holy, I beseech you by all your holy Names to kindly grant my prayer, weak as it is, to preserve me from all peril, and from the vexations and traps of the Demon, so that I may be delivered not only in the present, but forever. God of Abraham, God of Isaac, God of Jacob, God of the angels, God of the apostles, God of the martyrs, God of all the saints and the beloved of God, intercede on my behalf, for me N. God, so good, so kind, so gracious, so humble of heart, who desires not the death of the sinner, nor the downfall of his soul.

ORISON

*O God, whose mercy is infinite, I beg you most urgently, by the
strength and virtue of all the holy Names, which are inscribed or
written in this book, and by the names of all your holy Saints, to
graciously preserve me, N who am your creature, today and for all
time, as well as preserve from evil and iniquity all your creatures,
my friends and enemies, and all the faithful on the Earth. I beseech
you with all the humility of which a human creature is capable, by
the strength, virtue, and merit of the passion and death of Our Lord
Jesus Christ, by that of all your holy Names; and by the virtue of
the Blessed Virgin Mary, and all your saints, in this day and always
in whatever place I may be, to kindly keep me and my property
from the spite of my enemies, who seek only to destroy me: preserve
me, I say, from all perils, losses, thunders, storms, lightning, plague,
hunger, from snakes, as well as all terrible and dangerous beasts,
from danger of fire and water, and from sudden and eternal death,
so that we may all happily be safe and sound to praise, bless, and
glorify you, eternally for all centuries. Amen.*

Say the *Pater* and *Ave* in their entirety.

*Save us from the hands of our enemies, so that being delivered
from their hands, we may serve you without fear. Lord, the strength
of your arm is wondrously evident, you have exterminated a great
enemy, you have made manifest the greatness of your Glory, abasing the pride of the impious who raise themselves against you: the
fire of your anger that you have brought down upon their heads de-
vours them in the blink of an eye; the waters are heaped up, surging
one upon another, excited by the fury of your anger.*

Let horror and terror cut down their courage, at the idea alone of your strength. Lord, make them motionless, as stone, until your people have passed, and your Chosen are out of peril. Jesus Christ, King of Glory, is come; this God, who was made man, extirpated the armed band by the strength of His almighty arm. Yet, Jesus passing in the midst of them, went on His way. May the horror and terror cut down their courage, at the idea alone of your strength. Lord, make them motionless, as stone, until your people, and the people you have chosen, have passed.

ONE MUST SAY THIS THRICE, WHEN READY TO PASS WHERE his enemies are; it is said that Charlemagne used it in war, and thereby remained invincible; since those times, there was so much faith in the Orisons of the Holy Church, that cannon shot is avoided by saying the following Orison:

I entreat you, Stone, by blessed Saint Stephen, the first martyr, whom the accursed Jews stoned, yet who prayed for his persecutors and executioners, saying: Lord Jesus Christ, do not impute to them this fault, rather deign to forgive them for they know not what they do, in order that you cannot wound me, N, who am the servant of God.

ORISON AGAINST ARROWS

Which you may try against a dog or other beast, that cannot
be hit if it has this, or the following Orison,
worn around its neck.

I entreat you, Arrows, by the charity and flagellation of Our Lord
Jesus Christ, O arrows, remain ineffectual, I conjure you by Heaven
and Earth, by the stars and the planets: be, hence, null and void,
I conjure you by the sepulchre of Our Lord Jesus Christ. O arrow,
I command you, by the resurrection of Our Lord Jesus Christ, to
harm none. O arrow, I conjure you once more, by Heaven and by
Earth, by the stars in the heavens, and by all under the heavens and
upon the Earth, by the terrible Day of Judgment, by the virginity of
the divine body of Our Lord Jesus Christ, and by that of the glorious Virgin Mary, His mother, not to harm anyone whosoever he be.
O arrow, I order and command you, by the most Holy Trinity, to
remain ineffectual.

May the peace of Our Lord Jesus Christ be always with me, with
the power of the prophet Ely: O arrow, do not kill, remain without
effect, I entreat you by the virtue of the Blessed Virgin Mary, by the
head of John the Baptist, by the twelve apostles, by the four evangelists, by the martyrs, confessors, virgins and widows of God, by the
angels and archangels: O arrow, I make once more, the same prohibition, by the great living God, the true God, the holy God, by the
same God who from nothing made all things: O arrow, I reiterate
the same prohibition, by the Annunciation of Our Lord Jesus Christ:
O arrow, once more, I forbid you to wound or in any way harm me,
N, who am the servant of God, and by the ineffable memory of N. ✠

2 ✠ 1 ✠ q.g. 222. L.M. ✠ 1 ✠ Lord Jesus Christ. Alpha ✠ and Omega ✠ Emmanuel, may no sword pierce me, may I be born through Our Lord Jesus Christ, my guardian, my liberator and my Saviour, that no iron can have any effect on N, who is the servant of God.

May those who offend me feel the effect of your justice. Annihilate, Lord, those who draw near to attack me; take your weapons and your shield, raise yourself to come to my aid and deliverance, N, your servant. ✠ Amen. ✠ Tate Aîti ✠ Aît Ain ✠ may God preserve me from all evil, from danger, and from death, I, N, who am the servant of God. Amen. Jesus Christ conquers. ✠ Jesus Christ commands. ✠ Jesus Christ reigns. ✠ Jesus Christ leads. ✠ Jesus Christ be within me, may he break and shatter the iron which is turned against me: O arrow, I command you, by that spear of which I have spoken, to remain without any effect which is harmful to me, and may all the weapons of my enemies, seen or unseen, hold no threat for me, N, the servant of God.

WHOEVER CARRIES THIS ORISON HAS NOTHING TO FEAR, from arrows, swords, nor other weapons: none will be able to harm him; neither the Devil, if he has made a pact with him, nor magicians nor any others can harm him; he will be safe & sound in all places and at all times ✠ ✠ ✠. If, believing in this you venture forth, you will experience wonders; if you wear this Orison around your neck, no harm will come to you.

Barnasa ✠ Leutias ✠ Bucella ✠ Agla ✠ Agla ✠ Tetragrammaton ✠ Adonay ✠ Lord, great admirable God, help N, your servant as

unworthy as I am, ✠ deliver me from all danger, from the death of
the soul and the body, and from the snares of my enemies, seen and
unseen. ✠ God ✠ Ely ✠ Eloy ✠ Ela ✠ Adonay ✠ Sabaoth ✠ may
these holy names ✠ be propitious and salutory for me, N, the servant
of God, ✠ for this is my body, ✠ may he love me. ✠ Amen.

There are ten names by which God is called in whatever
place you may be, and by which it is said that the body
of Christ is in some way compelled and bound. They are
named in the Orison above.

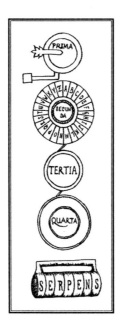

ORISON TO CONJURE ALL KINDS OF WEAPONS

I conjure you, all kinds of weapons which were used to put to death the holy martyrs, I command you to become without effect, or rather, I forbid you by all the merits of the martyrs, to have any power over me, neither to cut me in any part of my body, nor to shed even one drop of my blood, neither to wound nor injure me, in any place whatsover, I, N, who am a servant of God. ✠ Cross and Passion of Our Lord Jesus Christ, be in my recollection, and strengthen me against my enemies, ✠ your peace and blessing be always with me. O arrow, become useless for my enemies, and without effect, this I entreat you by the blessed Virgin Mary, by the head of John the Baptist, by the apostles, martyrs, confessors, virgins and widows, by the angels and archangels: ✠ O arrow, be without harmful effect in regard to me, by the Annunciation of Our Lord Jesus Christ: O arrow, I implore you by the crown of thorns which was placed on the sacred head of Our Lord Jesus Christ. ✠ O arrow, I repeat, by the capture and flagellation of Our Lord Jesus Christ, ✠ O arrow, by the nails which pierced the hands and feet of Our Lord Jesus Christ. O arrow, by the wounds of Our Lord Jesus Christ, His resurrection, I forbid you to injure me, I, N, who am the servant of God, ✠ in the name of the Father ✠ and of the Son ✠ and of the Holy Spirit. ✠ Amen.

ORISON TO JESUS CHRIST THE SAVIOUR

I beseech you, Lord, Son of the great living God, by your holy Cross, to forgive my sins, to keep my head safe and sound by your holy Cross, to guard my feet from all accidents by your precious Cross, and to preserve all my limbs; grant me, if it pleases you, forgiveness for my sins, and eternal life. ✠ *Holy God, sanctify me.* ✠ *Almighty God, strengthen me.* ✠ *God eternal, sustain me.* ✠ *Immortal God, have pity on me, N, who is your servant, for my sins are innumerable. I am not even worthy to be called your servant, on account of the offenses that I committed against your divine Majesty; this is why I implore you, O my God, to suffuse my soul and my heart with your divine Love; You, who live and reign eternally, in Heaven and on Earth. Amen.*

ANOTHER ORISON

My God, my Father, have pity on me. ✠ *O Son, O Holy Spirit, be with me: deliver me from my enemies.* ✠ *Sword, I conjure you, by the holy Priest of the Old Testament, who gave Mary entrance into the Temple, and to Our Lord Jesus Christ, saying: the sword of suffering has pierced Him to His soul so that you cannot wound me, N, who is the servant of God:* ✠ *I implore you, Stones, by blessed Saint Stephen, the first martyr, who the Jews stoned to death, not to wound me in any way, I, N, the servant of God.* ✠ *In the name of the Father, and of the Son, and of the Holy Spirit. Amen.*

HERE ARE THE WORDS SENT BY HOLY POPE LEO TO CHARLES, King of France & Emperor of the West: whoever shall carry them, read them or have them read, will not suffer any misfortune on that day, will be safeguarded from fire and water, will die with honour in old age, and will be well provided for; likewise, for a pregnant woman, she will have relief if she carries it on her.

Cross of Jesus Christ which I adore always: ✚ *may the Cross of Jesus Christ be my true salvation during my life and after my death:* ✚ *may the Cross of Jesus Christ render the sword of my adversaries useless against me;* ✚ *may the Cross of Jesus Christ free me from the bonds of Death.* ✚ *May the Cross of Jesus Christ be for me* ✚ *a wondrous sign;* ✚ *may the Cross of Jesus Christ be my power, authority and strength;* ✚ *may the Cross of Jesus Christ be my guarantee, my safeguard, and assure me of a beneficial success against my enemies;* ✚ *may the Cross of Jesus Christ deliver me from all peril, now and to come;* ✚ *may I obtain the succor of divine grace through this sign of the Cross, and may its authority and power be as a barrier and defense against my enemies;* ✚ *may the Cross of Jesus Christ deliver me from all adversity and misfortune in my life;* ✚ *may the Cross of Jesus Christ be always with me and save me: may it be before me and behind me, for as soon as the Demon, my old enemy, sees you before me and with me, he will withdraw and flee far from me;* ✚ *may all evil and unclean spirits flee and avoid me by this sign of the Cross* ✚ *Paix Heloy* ✚ *Tetragrammaton* ✚ *Diday* ✚ *Pontayeto Esbri* ✚ *Yet Jesus passing in the midst of them, went on His way* ✚ *Jesus* ✚ *Source* ✚ *Principle* ✚ *End* ✚ *Truth* ✚ *Almighty.* ✚ *In the name of the Father* ✚ *and of the Son* ✚ *and of the Holy Spirit.* ✚ *Amen.*

THESE ARE THE NAMES OF JESUS CHRIST

which were chosen and drawn from the Holy Scripture, and
if someone carries them, he will have great success & lose
nothing; also, wearing them around the neck
will make one loved by all.

✠ *Authos* ✠ *a nostro* ✠ *noxio* ✠ *Bay,* ✠ *Gloy* ✠ *Apen* ✠ *Agla* ✠
Agios ✠ *Hischiros.*

THESE ARE THE WORDS THAT ADAM SAID,

when he was in Hell or Limbo, or on the edge of Acheron. If
you carry them on yourself in war, you will not be killed by
anyone there; thus it is for the traveler who carries it for 70
days, he will not be taken on the road, nor attacked by rob-
bers, and will have time for a priest to hear his confession and
will have remission of his sins. It is also of great virtue for
those who travel on the sea. Those who carry it avoid peril, if
it is carried with great devotion.

✠ *Valeam de Zazac* ✠ *Adonay N (your name)* ✠✠✠✠✠ *Beginning*
✠ *and End* ✠ *Unction* ✠ *Wisdom* ✠ *Truth* ✠ *Hope* ✠ *Comforter* ✠ *It*
is I who am the Fountain ✠ *the Mediator* ✠ *Agios* ✠ *the Ewe* ✠ *the*
Bond ✠ *the Foot* ✠ *the Lion* ✠ *the Bread* ✠ *Telos* ✠ *the Hand* ✠ *the*
Stone ✠ *the Cornerstone* ✠ *the Blessed* ✠ *the Husband* ✠ *the Child,*
the Divinity ✠ *the Truthful* ✠ *the Darkness, the Grace* ✠ *Truth* ✠
Peace ✠ *the Source* ✠ *Atitay* ✠ *Love* ✠ *Alleluia* ✠ *Alleluia* ✠ *Alleluia*
✠ *Amen* ✠ *the Unity, the Strength* ✠ *the Last* ✠ *the Almighty* ✠
Matthew ✠ *John* ✠ *Mark* ✠ *Luke* ✠✠✠

The Sword[5]

MAY THESE HOLY NAMES BE FOR THE SALVATION OF MY SOUL, in the name of Jesus, Mary, and in the name of Saint Eloy; as worn by King Fabricius, and left to the King named Eloy. Thus carried, one can neither be taken nor killed; if one does not want to try this oneself, put them on an ox that the butcher wants to kill, and he will never be able to.

Pathay ✠ *Vey* ✠ *Adonay* ✠ *in the name of the Father* ✠ *and of the Son* ✠ *and of the Holy Spirit;* ✠ *Yet, Jesus passing in the midst of them, went on His way,* ✠ *O* ✠ *Var* ✠ *Adar* ✠ *Malarum terrarum*

negat ✠ the Word was made flesh, and lives amongst us. ✠ Christus
✠ Tetragrammaton ✠ which tells him that you succeed. ✠ Amen.
Six. ✠ Amen. It is I who am this Jesus you seek. If you see these
people who steal my people, you run at once to be their friends,
and you make yourself the accomplice of adulteries: there is nothing
but filth and spite on your lips, and your tongue is concerned only
with deftly betraying those who confide in you. ✠ And blessings are
poured upon your legacy. ✠ Praise God. ✠ ✠ ✠

ORISON OF SAINT AUGUSTINE ADDRESSED TO THE HOLY SPIRIT, WHICH IS SAID TO HAVE A REVELATION.

O my God, be propitious to me, I who am only an unworthy and
miserable sinner, deign to keep me and be with me continuously
throughout the course of my life, by night as well as by day. God of
Abraham, God of Isaac, God of Jacob, take pity on me, and send to
aid me your holy archangel Michael, to defend and protect me in
all my evils and perils. Blessed Saint Michael, deliver me from all
danger, even from the terrible Judgment of God: O blessed Saint
Michael, archangel, I implore you by the grace of which you are
worthy, by Our Lord Jesus Christ, the only Son of God, to deliver me
today from the danger of death: Saint Gabriel, Saint Raphael, and
all the holy angels of God, help me, I entreat all of you, as many as
you are in Heaven, to grant me your aid and your power, so that
none of my enemies, small as well as great, however they may be,
can make me feel neither the traits of their spite, nor their vengeance, neither on the road or on water, nor by fire, neither may they

contrive for me a sudden death, nor be contrary to me, whether I am sleeping or awake. Here is ✠ the cross of the Lord, thus flee, all my enemies! and disappear, you who seek to harm me, the Lion of the tribe of Judah prevailed, the race of David. Alleluia. Saviour of the world, save me, you who redeemed us by shedding your own blood on the tree of the Cross. We beg you most humbly, O my God, to help us. Agios, O Theios, Agios, Ischyros, Agios, Athanatos, Eleïson Himas, holy God, strong God, immortal God, have pity on us. Precious Cross of Jesus Christ, save us. Cross of Jesus Christ, protect us. Cross of Jesus Christ, defend us. In the name of the Father, and of the Son, and of the Holy Spirit. Amen.

Rhythm

ORISON OF SAINT CYPRIAN

Whoever recites this Orison, will be safeguarded
from all dangers and perils.

I, Cyprian, servant of Our Lord Jesus Christ, prayed to God the almighty Father, and said to him: You alone are the strong God, my almighty God who lives in Heaven, your abode filled with light, you are holy and praiseworthy, you have foretold the wickedness of your servant in all eternity, and the iniquities in which he is plunged by the power of the devil and I ignored your holy Name; I walked in the midst of the ewes and they left me at once, and the clouds could not pour rain upon the Earth, which was dry and arid, nor the trees bear fruit; and the women were pregnant. I sealed the passages of the Sea, and it was impossible to open them. I myself did all these evils, and again an infinity of others.

But now, my Lord Jesus Christ, my God, I know your holy Name, I love it and I repent with all my heart, and from the depths of my soul, the profusion of my wickedness, my iniquities and my crimes, and forthwith am resolute to abide in your Love, and to submit myself to your holy commandment, for you are the only and unique Word of the almighty God the Father. I implore you now, my God, to break the bonds of the clouds, unbind them, let fall upon the Earth and upon your children, a soft and gentle rain, to bring forth food for them, as well as for the animals who live in the water, releasing the rivers that I constrained with all the rest. I entreat you, my God, by your holy Name. My God, keep me, N, who am your creature, from danger, ✛ and from all evil; ✛ I ask this of you by your holy Name, to which all things, spiritual and corporeal, owe honour and

glory. And by Emmanuel, which means: God is in us; and say to
the waters, I have sanctified the ports and places where you will
pass: and you have delivered, Lord, the children of Israël from the
captivity of the Pharaoh: also deign to deliver me from all evil, peril,
and danger. I entreat you, I, N, who has the joy of belonging to
you being your creature, by your servants Moses and Aaron, extend
over me N, your right hand and pour your holy blessing on me. You
are my God, bless me as you have your good Angels, that is to say,
the Angels and Archangels, of Thrones, Dominations, Principalities,
Powers, Virtues, Cherubim and Seraphim. Deign also to bless me,
N, my Lord Jesus Christ; I who am your creature, bless me in such a
way that no impure spirit or demon can do me harm, that I cannot
receive any blemish, that neither their evil deeds nor their wicked
designs, neither their evil eye nor poisoned tongue, nor any persecution on their behalf, can hold any threat for me.

Keep far from us, Lord, all evil and every malign spirit; may all
evil men and pernicious women withdraw far from us and flee us,
as we avoid them, may all enemies and adversaries recoil from us,
that they do not threaten or have power over us. We ask this of you
by the virtue of the Most High, and if somebody, Lord, wants to
harm me or do the least evil to me, place me my God, under your
holy protection, I, N, who am your creature, and deign to do good to
me. I ask this of you by the virtue and merits of all your holy angels,
who praise you unceasingly; and by all your patriarchs, your apostles, the saints in Paradise, deliver and preserve your servant from
the malicious glances of all my enemies, and alike from those who
could harm me. Amen.

I beg you once more, my Lord Jesus Christ, by all the holy prayers which are said throughout the churches of Christendom, to liberate me and deliver me from the malevolence of all evil deeds, and from all the malifices that can be perpetrated by demons and by evil men and women. I ask this of you in the names of the Cherubim and Seraphim, that they not have any power or influence over us. I beg you most humbly, God the Father, most gentle and merciful, by your Annunciation, your Death and your sepulchre, by your admirable and marvelous Ascension, by the coming and the arrival of the Holy Spirit on Earth, and by the prayers of all the saints, by the penitence of all the holy pilgrims, by the beauty of Adam, by the sacrifice of Abel, by the deliverance of Noah, by the faith of Abraham, by the offering of Isaac, by the religion of Melchizedek, by the humility of Job, by the holy love of Moses, by the sacrifice of Abraham, by the religion of Aaron and by the psalms of David, by the annunciation of Isaac, by the tears of Jeremiah, by the contrition of Zachariah, and by the depth of the abyss of Hell, by the heights of Heaven, by the splendour of the Divinity, by the tongues of the apostles, by the ways of the evangelists and the angels, by that which Moses saw, by the radiance of the lights, by the holy discourses and sermons of the apostles, by the baptism of Our Lord Jesus Christ, by the voice of the Heavenly Father which resounds from His throne and is heard upon the Earth: This is my beloved Son, in whom I have put all my kindness. Listen to what He will say to you; and by the miracle, when Jesus Christ sated the five thousand in the desert from five fish and two loaves of bread, and by He who resurrected Lazarus, and by all those who fear God.

I beg you, Lord, to break all these bonds, and preserve me from the charms of their eyes, I, N, who am the servant of God; I entreat you, Lord, by all these holy deeds, and by all the virtues written in this book in praise and honour of the great living God, not to allow them influence over me, N, your servant. May this Great God, I say, who created all things, not allow their magic, enchantments or malefica, if they used it, having influence over gold, silver, bronze, iron, or on that which is finely wrought, chiselled or rough, or silks and wools, or on linens and fabrics or stuff made from these materials, on all the bones of men and women, of fish, on wood, or on any other thing whatever it is, or on herbs, over books or papers or virgin parchments; if they put it or had it put on some stone, on water, or wine, or bread, or cheese, or within the Earth, or on the Earth, or on the sepulchre of some giant,[6] or Hebrew, or Pagan, or Christian, or in the hair, or on the hair, the clothes, the shoes, some strap or belt, and in or on whatever it may be, that's to say, in some place or thing that all these evil deeds are done or must be done. I ask and most humbly entreat you, by the virtue of the almighty God the Father, and of the Son, and of the Holy Spirit, to destroy them and render them null and void, that they may have no power over me ✠ N, who am your servant. I beg you by the merits of Saint Cyprian.

Archangel Saint Gabriel

While one carries this Orison, one is under the protection of the Archangels Michael, Gabriel and Raphael, of all the Saints and Elect of God or predestined, by all the Orders of the blessed Saints, and by this traveler who was crucified.

O my God, my sovereign while I, N, am your creature, deliver me from all malefice, from every peril and evil, from the pernicious tongue and eyes of my enemies who seek to destroy me. O God the almighty and eternal Father, deliver me from the dangers which surround me, as you delivered the three children, Shadrach, Meshach and Abednego, from the flames of the fire; deliver also your servant from all peril and danger, of the soul as much as of the body.

HERE ARE THE NAMES OF JESUS CHRIST

Whoever wears them while travelling, on the Earth or by Sea, will be preserved from all kinds of dangers and perils, if they are said with faith and devotion.

Trinity ✠ Agios ✠ Sother ✠ Messiah ✠ Emmanuel ✠ Sabaoth and Adonay ✠ Athanatos ✠ Jesus ✠ Pentagna ✠ Agiagon ✠ Ischyros ✠ Eleïson ✠ O Theos ✠ Tetragrammaton ✠ Ely ✠ Saday ✠ Eagle ✠ great Man ✠ Sight ✠ Flower ✠ Spring ✠ Saviour ✠ Alpha ✠ and Omega ✠ the Firstborn ✠ Wisdom ✠ Virtue ✠ Comforter ✠ Way ✠ Truth ✠ and Life ✠ Intercessor ✠ Doctor ✠ Salvation ✠ Lamb ✠ Ewe ✠ Calf ✠ Hope ✠ Ram ✠ Lion ✠ Worm ✠ Mouth ✠ Speech ✠ or Word ✠ Splendour ✠ Sun ✠ Glory ✠ Light ✠ Image ✠ Bread ✠ Doorway ✠ Peter ✠ Spouse ✠ Shepherd ✠ Prophet ✠ Priest ✠ Saint

✠ *Immortal* ✠ *Jesus Christ* ✠ *Father* ✠ *Son* ✠ *Holy Man* ✠ *God* ✠
Agios ✠ *Resurrection* ✠ *Miscbios* ✠ *Charity* ✠ *Eternity* ✠ *Creator* ✠
Redeemer ✠ *Unity* ✠ *Supreme Being* ✠ *Evam* ✠.

HERE ARE THE NAMES OF THE BLESSED VIRGIN

Life ✠ *Virgin* ✠ *Flower* ✠ *Cloud* ✠ *Queen* ✠ *Theotokos* ✠ *All* ✠ *the*
Silent ✠ *Imperatrix* ✠ *Peace loving* ✠ *Mistress* ✠ *Earth* ✠ *Birth*
✠ *Fountain* ✠ *Well* ✠ *Way* ✠ *Woman* ✠ *Dawn* ✠ *Moon* ✠ *Sun* ✠
Doorway ✠ *Home* ✠ *Temple* ✠ *Blessed* ✠ *Glorious* ✠ *Pious* ✠ *Court*
✠ *Source* ✠ *End* ✠ *School* ✠ *Ladder* ✠ *brilliant Star* ✠ *Grape* ✠
Vine ✠ *Tower* ✠ *Grail* ✠ *Redemptrix* ✠ *Liberatrix* ✠ *Arch* ✠ *Bed* ✠
Cinnamon ✠ *Generation* ✠ *Woman* ✠ *Friend* ✠ *Valley* ✠ *Gorge* ✠
Trumpet ✠ *Thorn* ✠ *beautiful Stone* ✠ *Mother* ✠ *Alana* ✠ *Lovely*
✠ *Rose* ✠ *blessed Door* ✠ *Free* ✠ *Town* ✠ *Dove* ✠ *Pomegranate* ✠
Tabernacle ✠ *Great* ✠ *Mary* ✠ *Amen. In honour of God and the*
blessed Saint Cyprian. Praise be to God. Amen.

ORISON OF SAINT MICHAEL
For those who travel on water.
It is also useful against sheep pox.

Archangel Michael, who guards Paradise, come to help the people of
God, and be inclined to defend us against the Demon, and all of our
most powerful enemies, and who lead us into the presence of God,
the abode of the blessed.

Lord, my God, I will sing your praises in the presence of your angels. I will pay you my most humble homage in your holy Temple, and will make known the greatness of your Name.

THE PRESENT FIGURE IS THE MEASURE OF THE WOUND IN THE SIDE OF JESUS CHRIST

Whoever wears it need not fear any trap from his enemies, seen or unseen; and a pregnant woman in labour, will have prompt help, provided only that she sees it. It will give you victory over your enemies, safeguard you from ruin, injury or sudden death. Write it on virgin parchment with a pen and ink never before used, on Holy Friday, one hour after midnight, having previously recited the Passion, and once the Figure is made, scent it with a good perfumes, and then carry it on oneself.

172

OF THE CONSTRUCTION OF THE PENTACLE
& TOOLS OF THE ARTE

 HE TWO PENTACLES, gíven here,[7] are of a potent virtue to bind and constrain the more
resolute spiríts; this is their sentence and
their condemnation: as soon as you show
them, they will not cause any trouble and
obey you in all things. It should be noted that no powerful
or potent book of magic can be made that does not have
these pentacles imprinted therein. They must be made on
exorcised and blessed virgin goat parchment, over which
a Mass of the Holy Spirít has been said, after which, make
the Pentacle on a Wednesday night, in the hour of Mercury. *Nota* – The ink and the quill must have been exorcised
or they will be of no use. You must be alone, in a solítary
and chaste place, and must have been pure and clean for

three days prior, both inside and outside; the same conduct must be observed in all other operations. After making the circle, bless it, sprinkling holy water over it and saying: *Asperges me ... etc.* After the Pentacles are made, one must cense them with aromatic perfumes, then place them in a clean, earthenware vessel, where they must remain for three days and three nights; then wrap them in pure white linen, in order to carefully conserve them – lest they be profaned – until you place them in some book, which must then be censed and exorcised, and then kept in a pure place, and open it only when necessary.

PRAYER BEFORE ANY OPERATION

O almighty God, most strong God, gentle God, most high and glorious God, sovereign and just God, O God full of grace and clemency, I throw myself at your feet, I, N, who am an unworthy sinner and filled with iniquity: I present myself before your Majesty, I implore your forgiveness and your bounty. Do not look at the infinite multitude of my sins, since you have compassion always for the penitent, deign to answer my prayers; bless, I beg you, my operation by your infinite bounty, your mercy, and your almighty virtue. This is the grace for which I ask you ✠ in the name of your Son ✠ who reigns with you and the Holy Spirit ✠ in this century and all other centuries. Amen.

Afterwards, say the *Pater* and the *Ave* five times.

EXORCISMS OF THE PARCHMENT, INK & QUILL

I exorcise you, impure ſpiriꞇ, ſpiriꞇ of illusion, so that in the Name of God almighty you can do naught but wiꞇhdraw from this operation, and that all your profaniꞇy being far from us, these things that we exorcise will remain sanꞔꞇified. In the Name of the Father, ✛ of the Son ✛ and of the Holy Spiriꞇ. Amen. So that, I, N, by the virtue of these perfumes, may be sustained by all the virtue of the Spiriꞇ of God, and that no illusion can harm me, this I aſk by the great and formidable Name of God, Shemhamphoraſh.

BLESSING OF THE PERFUME

God of Abraham, ✛ God of Isaac, ✛ God of Jacob, ✛ bless this creature, N (name of perfume), may the strength and the virtue of its scent be intensified, so that iꞇ can hold the ſpiriꞇs I must invoke through the perfeꞔꞇion of my work and my desire; I aſk this of you by your Son, Our Lord Jesus Christ, who liꞣes and reigns wiꞇh you in uniꞇy wiꞇh the Holy Spiriꞇ, now and forever. Amen.

EXORCISM OF THE FIRE

Having put the fire in an earthenware vessel, say over iꞇ:
I exorcise you, creature of fire, by He who made and created all things, so that all phantoms who could harm me, wiꞇhdraw far from you.

God of Abraham ✠ *God of Isaac* ✠ *God of Jacob,* ✠ *bless this creature, N, so that being blessed and sanctified in honour of your holy Name, it drives away from those who carry it or see it, all phantoms or harmful enemies. This we ask of you, by your holy Son, Our Lord Jesus Christ, who lives and reigns in Heaven with you in unity with the Holy Spirit, now and forever. Amen.*

THE VIRTUES OF THE SEVEN PSALMS
& ORISONS AFOREMENTIONED

THE GOSPEL ACCORDING TO JOHN

T IS PERFORMED in order to safeguard oneself against all accidents during the day, being recîted in the morning upon rising, sprinkling one's face wîth holy water while saying: *Asperges me ...* &c. After, crouch against the wall so as not to be seen, strike your chest three times saying, *Confiteor*, &c., then stand up and recîte the Gospel. Remain in your room for half an hour, recîting the *Seven Psalms*, the *Lîtanies of the Saints*, and the *Our Father*.

If one carries the aforesaid Gospel on oneself, wrîtten on virgin parchment wîth a goose quill on the first Sunday of the year, one hour before the sun rises, one will be invulnerable and safeguarded against many ills.

AGAINST ALL KINDS OF CHARMS

The seven mysterious Orisons, one for each day of the week, are meant to counter all kinds of dangers, evils, misfortunes and accidents: see page 134 and the Mysterious Orison that follows.

To make use of the seven Orisons ît is necessary, on the first Tuesday of the Moon before the Sun rises, to gíve alms to the first beggar that you meet in the Church where you hear Mass. Then when you return, recîte the aforesaid Orisons and wrîte them on virgin parchment; the crosses therein must be wrîtten wîth blood drawn from the middle finger of your left hand, and wîth each cross that you draw you must make one over yourself. After that, you must bless and cense the Orisons, and thus, carrying them on yourself, you will be protected from all the traps of your enemies.

AGAINST THE ADVERSITIES OF THE WORLD

This Orison will destroy enchantments, &c. and must be accompanied by that of the Virgin, also on p. 142, and the Orison of Great Virtue, p. 143. These three Orisons are wrîtten on Monday at midnight, wîth a candle of yellow wax on the table to illuminate them; before wrîting pronounce the following: *You shall tread boldly on the asp and on the basilisk, you will bruise the lion and the dragon!* Then boldly write these Orisons on virgin parchment of an exorcised roe-deer and, carrying them on yourself, it is possible to overthrow, subdue and destroy your enemies; the first of these Orisons is used to charm weapons.

ORISON OF GREAT VIRTUE

To make use of this Orison, one must write it on virgin parchment the first Monday of the Moon before sunrise. The parchment must have been exorcised and have had three Masses of the Holy Spirit said over it, on three successive Mondays. Go afterwards to gather vervain – on a Friday in the hour of Venus. It is necessary, when one is near the herb, to extend the left hand over it, your face turned toward the East, then say: *facta isquina fatos jaara. Herb, whose virtue is admirable and produces wonderful effects, I pick you so that you serve me in what I wish.*

Pliny, the Naturalist, says that magicians claim that this herb must be picked towards the beginning of the Dog Days, without the action being seen by the sun or the moon, having beforehand made atonement to the earth with a buried offering of honeycomb and honey; after, a circle must be drawn with iron around the plant and then it should be pulled up with the left hand and not allowed to touch the earth. The leaves, stem and root must be dried separately in the shade. Place them all on the aforementioned parchment, and wrap the whole in a piece of white satin.

Carry the herb on oneself in the manner just taught and you will have all you ask for; you cannot be refused in marriage to a girl, regardless of how wealthy she is; but you must refrain from cursing, and nor should you visit places of debauchery while carrying this herb, or it would become unfruitful. Moreover, every morning before the sunrise, you must say the Orison, with a *Pater* and an *Ave*.

AGAINST HUMAN FRAILTY

This Orison is used to see what you wish for in a dream. When you feel about to succumb or be weak in whatever matter, recite the Orison, and that which follows it, making the sign of the cross as many times as there are in writing it. Write them down on the first Friday of the Moon, an hour before sunrise; the crosses must be marked in blood drawn from the thumb on the left hand, all on virgin parchment.

When you want to perform an operation, put these Orisons under the pillow, on the side that you normally sleep; it's best to place them under your left ear, and you will see the effect that you wish for.

ORISON: O LORD JESUS CHRIST

To make use of this Orison, it should be written on Tuesday at eleven in the evening; the crosses marked with blood drawn from the index finger of the left hand. It is used to discover the accomplices of a crime or a theft.

Nota – It should be written on virgin parchment, and you must have neither eaten nor drunk for seven hours. The following day, Wednesday, you may eat or drink only after the sun sets, after which, place the Orison beneath your head upon retiring; and by experience you will know the effect of the request. It is of use against enemies, if you add the Orison beginning: *However, Jesus passing in the midst of them*... from the Orison against Enemies, page 132.

VERY USEFUL ORISON FOR THOSE WHO TRAVEL

It is necessary to write it on virgin parchment three days before departure, before sunrise, reciting beforehand Psalm 125: *In convertendo* ... The crosses are to be marked in blood drawn from the little finger of the left hand; two of these crosses are drawn with blessed charcoal with the left hand; then Psalm 58 must be recited: *Deus, in nomine tuo salvum me fac.* By carrying the Orison on yourself, you will be feared and dreaded by your enemies, by magicians as much as by evil spirits, thieves and others; and you will receive what you request in your journeys. You will cause fear in all who wish you ill.

EXHORTATION TO JESUS CHRIST

You will write these holy names on virgin parchment on such day as you wish, before sunrise and make the crosses with your own blood, drawn from the little finger of the left hand, and afterwards cense, perfume and carry it on you with reverance, and you will be preserved from all danger.

TO MAKE A WOMAN FAITHFUL

Begin by writing the crosses of this Orison on common paper with ordinary ink; then write them with the left hand on virgin parchment, and also the pentacle *Adonay, Job, Magister, dicit* (page 140), with blessed charcoal on the first Monday of the Moon, and in the hour of the Moon. Then throw the paper into the fire, saying: *May you burn forever and not come with me to Judgment.* After, carry the parchment on yourself; and later, write the Orison on red paper. On Tuesday, in the hour of Mars, make the crosses in black ink, which has never been used and into which you have added three drops of blood drawn from the middle finger of the right hand. Carrying this Orison on yourself ensures that the woman will be faithful unto death.

THE GREAT HOLY POPE, LEO

One must write this Orison, on Sunday at the hour of the
Sun, on virgin parchment, first making the sign of the
cross, and all those you find should be marked with blood
drawn from the little finger of the left hand, and making as
many crosses over oneself as there are on the parchment; it
is necessary to recite Psalm 50. By carrying this parchment
on oneself you will receive from elders and princes what
you desire.

THE ORISON: I ENTREAT YOU, STONE

It is used to be invincible, fortunate in a fight, a siege and
to take an enemy camp. This Orison, with the two which
follow, must be written on virgin parchment, on Thursday at eleven o'clock in the evening. The crosses must be
made with blood, without making the sign of the cross.
One must, above all else, say the Psalm: *Judica Deus, nocentes*
and the Orison: *Obsecro te, Deus ...* One should not omit the
figures and characters which are the calculation of the Demon of Jupiter, which dominates the planet Venus. The
characters, L.M. are the names of Limoch and Machel, of
which one controls the winds on the Earth, and the other
stops lightning and storms; by these characters one can
raise hidden treasures noiselessly, delivering them to the
appointed place at the hour above (all things being observed

as indicated); carry the parchment, between midnight and one o'clock, to a three-way crossroads, where you make a circle with a pit in the middle, then the parchment – wrapped in a clean linen cloth – is placed in it and covered by an earthenware dish. Recite the aforementioned Orisons, and those which are under the dish will conjure spirits, restrain their impetuosity and bridle them.

If one performs the operation on Easter Saturday, the outcome will be more certain. The crosses should be marked in common charcoal; they are removed three days later at the same hour, they will serve you in all you desire.

ORISON TO COUNTER ALL CHARMS & POISONS

It is necessary to write this Orison, on Wednesday at the hour of Mercury, on paper soaked in the blood of a goat that has been left to dry for one day. The first cross should be done with the left hand, all the remainder with the right, with ink and quill that have never previously been used. Put three drops of the goat's blood into the ink; having finished, make three signs of the cross, recite Psalm 44, then carry the Orison on yourself, and do not be afraid, because marble will no longer be more durable than you.

HERE ARE THE WORDS OF POPE LEO III,
SENT TO CHARLEMAGNE

To make use of this Orison, you must fast for three days before wrîting ît. On the fourth day, before the rising of the sun and having said your prayers to God, recîte Psalm 50; then wrîte this Orison on blessed virgin parĉhment, after whiĉh you scent ît wîth fine perfume, and wrap ît in blessed whîte satin, and carry ît on yourself.

HERE ARE THE NAMES OF JESUS CHRIST, ETC.

This Orison is of great virtue, causing you to be loved, or bringing you whosoever you desire. Before wrîting ît, one needs to fast for three days, and to have three Masses said for the most forsaken soul; eaĉh time one leaves home to say Mass, ît is necessary to gîve alms to the first beggar you meet. Next, on the first Friday of the Moon at six o'cloĉk in the morning, recîte the Psalm: *Princîpes, the princes have persecuted me*, etc. Then wrîte the Orison on virgin parĉhment wîth a quill and ink never before used. Once ît is wrîtten, recîte whilst standing the Psalm: *Magnificat*, then cense the Orison, and carry ît on oneself. When one wants to make a person come to you, thrice recîte the Orison on that day, after whiĉh says: *May you come here as soon as possible, N* (say the person's first and surnames).

THESE ARE THE WORDS OF ADAM

In order for this Orison to serve you, you must recîte ît three times on the first Thursday of the crescent Moon before the rising of the sun, and another three times before you go to bed, in the hour of Jupîter. And on the following day, Friday, at the time of Venus, wrîte ît on a sheet of exorcised whîte paper wîth ink and a new pen; after whidh you recîte Psalm 118: *Immaculati omnes.* You then cense ît and carry ît on yourself. Above the aforesaid Orison, wrîte: *Valeam da Zarac.* ✠ That done, the Orison will enable you to enter into the good favour of princes and great lords, hosts and parents.

THAT THESE HOLY NAMES, ETC.

This is the Orison of Saint Alosée: *Pathay...* etc. One must wrîte this Orison on paper on Friday at 11 o'clodk in the evening, having said prior to that these holy names. You will soon see your enemies coming to pay homage to you.

ORISON OF SAINT CYPRIAN

Before wrîting ît, ît is necessary to fast for three days and confess; then recîte the following: *O Lord, enlighten me on this day on which I write the sentence of the demons; purify me, O my God, who lives and reigns in this time and for all time. So be it.*

Write it on virgin parchment, on a Sunday in the hour of the Sun. Then cense it and wrap it in clean fine linen. Once this is done, when one wishes to see the effect, fast for three days and confess, as above. This is of great virtue to invoke and bind demons.

HERE ARE THE HOLY NAMES

One writes this Orison on virgin parchment on such day as one wishes, before sunrise. Mark the signs of the cross in blood drawn from the little finger of the left hand, then cense it and carry it on yourself.

HERE ARE THE NAMES OF THE BLESSED VIRGIN

Write this Orison on virgin parchment; the crosses are marked in blood drawn from the ring finger of the left hand. This is done on the day one wishes, before the sun rises. Cense it and recite all the offices of the Conception, and carry it on yourself. It is used to obtain the graces of the Blessed Virgin.

ORISON OF SAINT MICHAEL

It is used against sheep pox, and by those who travel by
water, to be preserved from traps and pitfalls, temptations,
and the bites of poisonous beasts. Write the Orison on virgin parchment before sunrise on the day of Michaelmas;
cense it, and carry it on yourself in the honor of God and
Saint Cyprian.

CONJURATION FOR THE SPIRITS OF THE AIR,
To the angels ruling the Air on this day,
and imploring their aid in this way.

*I conjure you and beseech you to be favorable to me, and to listen
to the requests I wish you to carry out, and to come promptly to my
aid, and to help me and lead the operation which I am beginning to
a felicitous success, and I shall be obliged to you.*

That finished, you say: *I conjure you, O Angels, as many as
you are in all (naming each Angel), and compel you by the throne
of the great God, Adonay, Agios, O Theos, Ischyros, Athanatos,
Paraclytus, Alpha and Omega, and by the three sacred Names of
God, Agla, On, Tetragrammaton, to accomplish today what I desire.*

You then say the Conjuration of the assigned day, which
you will find in the *Grimoire of Pope Honorius*, after having
done the above. If the spirits, after the appropriate conjuration for the assigned day, remain obstinate, heeding neither the prayers nor the orders which will have been made

to them on behalf of the great living God, the Master of
the operation will make and recite the following exorcism:

ORISON

*Amerula, Tancha, Latiston, Zabac, Jancha, Escha, Aladia, Alpha and
Omega, Leiste, Oriston, Adonay, my heavenly Father, most clement, have pity on me, miserable sinner that I am. Extend the arm of
your omnipotence over me on this day, and strengthen me against
obstinate spirits, so that in consideration of your Divine magnifi-
cence, I may be endowed with wisdom, to praise and glorify your
holy Name. Thus I beseech you, my Lord and my God, and call on
you from from the depths of my heart so that, by your irrevocable
judgment, the spirits which I call are obliged to come and to bring
what I request, every time I invoke them, and to give true answers
to all I ask them, with damage neither to me nor any creature accompanying me, nor any other whosoever he is; and without detri-
ment to my life, nor to my spirits, nor my natural senses, and so
leaving me and my companions the full freedom of our five senses, without inspiring any horror or fear in me, without noise and
without furore, they will come to answer me in truth all I ask of
them. Through you, my Creator and my God, who lives and reigns
in eternity.*

DISMISSAL

I conjure you, Spirit N, such as you are, to leave me in peace and ease, and go to the place God bound you for all eternity. By Our Lord Jesus Christ, who lives and reigns now and for eternity. Amen. I grant you leave and demand that you appear before me every time that I call, only by the words of your name and stamping thrice upon the ground, to fulfil my will and desire.

THE WHITE PATER NOSTER TO GO INFALLIBLY TO HEAVEN

A succinct white Pater Noster that God made, that God said, that God put in Paradise. In the evening, as I went to bed, three angels lying there I found, one at the foot, two at the head and the good Virgin amid, who told me to lay down and doubt no more. The Good God is my Father, the good Virgin my Mother, the three apostles my brothers, and the three virgins my sisters. The shirt of God around my body is wrapped, and the cross of Saint Margaret on my chest writ. My Lady passed crying over the fields of God and there my Lord Saint John met: "O my Lord John, from whence have you come?" "I've come from Ave Salus." "Then you've not seen the Good God, for he was on the tree of the Cross if you did, his feet hanging and his hands nailed, and a crown of hawthorn upon His head."

Whosoever will say it thrice in the morning will attain Paradise in the end.

MYSTICAL SECRETS

TO STOP THE COURSE OF FIRE BURNING A HOUSE

Say: *May it stop, may it stop. I have hoped in you, Lord, whose glory mingles in eternity.*

Alternatively

Make three crosses on the mantelpiece with charcoal and write: *In te, Domine speravi, non confundar in æternum.*

TO GUARANTEE FIREARMS

Say three times: *God has a share in this, as does Our Lady. I see the mouth of the musket, God watches over the entrance and the Devil the exit.*

FOR LOVE

Take a four leaf clover and place it on an altar stone; let a Mass be said over it, then put it in a fragrant bouquet that you offer to the person you want to be loved by, saying: *Gabriel illa sunt.*

TO CURE COLIC

Put your large finger on your naval, and say: *Distress which is joined to me, or colic suffering which is between my liver and my heart, my spleen and my lungs, I stop you in the name of the Father,* ✠ *and of the Son* ✠ *and of the Holy Spirit,* ✠. And recite three *Pater* and three *Ave*, then name the patient, saying: *God has healed you.*

TO STOP A CARRIAGE OR CART

It is necessary to put a small stick in the middle of the road, with the following words written on it: *Jerusalem omnipotens Deus.* After, cross the road where the carriage or cart must pass.

TO WIN AT GAMBLING

Gather bracken on St John's Eve at midday; make a bracelet of it, in the form of the characters: HUTY.

GARTER FOR WALKING
which safeguards against all perils & dangers.

Take fine cloth of scarlet and from it make a garter to go around the knee, and from this hang nine hairs; after, buy some white satin of the same length, on which write with your blood: *verbum caro factum est et habitavit in nobis.* Put the satin on the scarlet, so the words touch the hair; put the garter over your left knee, the satin against your skin, and depart. As soon as one arrives, remove the garter to use again when needed; dust your bed wîth sugar and waŝh the soles of your feet wîth wine.

TO PREVENT A HUNTER FROM SHOOTING & KILLING

Say: *Si ergo me quæretis, finîte.*

TO BE EXEMPT FROM MILITARY SERVICE

Say: *Lord, you who never willed that your robe was rent, though ît was thrown out, do me the grace, I who draw my lot today, that I am exempt; Lord, grant me exemption; Lord, grant me exemption; if ît pleases you.* Then thrice recîte the *Pater*, etc.

TO BRING PEACE BETWEEN PEOPLE WHO FIGHT

Wrîte these ĉharaĉters around an apple: HAON, and throw ît into the thiĉk of the fight.

TO STOP BLEEDING

Say: ✠✠✠ *consummatum* ✠✠✠ *resurrexît* ✠✠✠ on the place.

TO HEAL A BURN

Say thrice over the burn, eaĉh time breathing over ît: *fire of God, lose your heat as Judas lost his colour when he betrayed Our Lord in the Garden of Olîves.*

TO CHASTISE THE INSOLENT

On Saturday morning, before sunrise, cut a wand from a virgin coppiced hazel, saying: *I cut you, this Summer's branch, in the name of N who I intend to harm.* Then, put a cover on the table, saying: ✠ *In nomine Patris* ✠ *et Filii* ✠ *et Spirîtus Sancti.* Say this three times with the following: *ad populum phaleras, ego te intus et in cute novi* ✠ *Drock* ✠ *Mirroch* ✠ *Essenaroth* ✠ *Betu* ✠ *Barac* ✠ *Maaroth.* Then say: *Holy Trinîty, punish he who did this evil to me and remove it by your great justice* ✠ *Eson* ✠ *Elion* ✠ *Esmaris,* and with the last words, strike the cover, and the intended person will receive the same blows; (by cover is meant a garment or a rug etc...). Note, that if you cut a wand from said hazel tree with the intention of mutilating someone's limb, it is necessary to say so when cutting it and, when you wish to heal the person, cut another wand from the tree with this intent, and do as above with the aim of healing, and it will infallibly heal. When you want to subject some other person to the same predicament, just say: *Holy Trinîty, punish N.* ✠ *Eson* ✠ *Elion* ✠ *Esmaris.* With the names of these Angels, strike as above, with the appropriate wand, and note that these wands can be used always; but, no-one should have cut any wand from that hazel previously.

TO PUT AN END TO HAIL & STORMS
STIRRED UP BY MALEFICA

Make the sign of the cross against the lightning, hail,
thunder and storm. Then take three hailstones from the
first falls, and throw them into the fire in the name of
the Trinity, and having said the *Pater* two or three times,
recite the *Gospel of Saint John*; that accomplished, make the
sign of the cross against the cloud and the thunder in all
directions, and mark the same salutory sign on the Earth,
towards the four quarters of the world; after three times
saying: *verbum caro est factum*, add as many times: *per Evangelica dicta fugiat tempestas ista.*

TO CURE ULCERS

First prepare the compress, whereof you make two pieces
that you form into a cross and over which you recite the
following three times: *God was born on Christmas Eve; God
died; God is resurrected; God orders that the wounds close; that the
pain passes; that the blood stops; and that it has neither substance
nor feeling, as did the five wounds of Our Lord Jesus Christ. In nomine Patris ✠ et Filii ✠ et Spiritus Sancti. ✠ Amen.* That done,
carry it to the table, then suck on the sore three times.
Take oil and thrice say over it: *Natus est Christus ✠ Mortuus
est Christus ✠ Resurrexit Christus ✠.* Then take it in the mouth
and blow it on the sore, apply the compress and, if the
ulcer is drawn out, it should be done again.

TO LIFT ALL SPELLS & ENCHANTMENTS

Take a sheep's heart and pierce it with nails.[8] Hang it in
the chimney, saying: *Rostin Clasta, Auvara, Chasta, Custodia,
Duranée.* It is necessary to say these same words over the
heart; and the eighth day will not come to pass without
the sorcerer who cast the spell coming to beg you to release
the heart, because he feels great pains in his chest; then,
you ask him to lift his spell, and he will ask you to throw
him some animal, which you can grant him, otherwise his
heart will burst in his body.

TO DISCOVER A THIEF

Write separately on pieces of paper the names of all those
who are in the house, masters, servants and others. Throw
them into a bronze pan filled with clear water; then say
over it: *I conjure you, Onazarde, Arogani, Labilafs, Parandomo,
Azigola, Maractatam, Siranday, Eptaleton, Lamboured, to reveal
the thief to me.* Then, if the thief's name is in the pan, it will
rise to the surface of the water, and if two or more come
up, they are accomplices.

AGAINST THE FLOW OF BLOOD

Say: *Anna peririt Mariam, Elizabeth peririt Joannem. Maria autem Christum. In nomine Jesu cesset sanguis ab hoc famulo, vel ab
hac famula.*

FOR A LAMED HORSE

Say: *Pater noster*, etc. until *in cœlo et in terra. In nomine Patris, et Filii, et Spiritus Sancti. Amen. In honour of God and Saint Eloy.*[9]

FOR CANKER THAT AFFLICTS SHEEP

White canker, black canker, red canker, canker of all kinds, I conjure you not to have any more hold over this herd, as the Devil has over the Priest when he says the holy Mass.

AGAINST DISEASES & INJURIES

I know a sergeant in the village who says the following Orison over all the ill and injured who present themselves to him requesting that he say it: *In the name of the Father, and of the Son, and of the Holy Spirit. Saint Anne, who gave birth to the Virgin Mary, the Virgin Mary who gave birth to Jesus Christ. God blesses and heals you, poor creature N, of relapse, injury, fractures, nerve disorders and handicaps, and of any wound whatever it may be. In the honour of God, the Virgin Mary, Saint Cosmas and Saint Damian. Amen.* Then do three *Pater* and three *Ave*.

What is remarkable is that this Orison, so eloquent and so spiritual as it is, has healed almost everyone for whom it has been said, as has been attested to by many people of faith.

TO HEAL DISEASES OF THE EYE

As Saint John was passing through there were three virgins in his path, and to them he said: *What are you doing here?* They answered: *We are healing cataracts in the eyes. O heal, virgins, heal the eyes of N.* Making the sign of the cross while blowing on the eye, he went on: *Cataract, inflammation, scratches, migraines, and spider bites, I order you to have no more power over this eye than the Jews had over the body of Our Lord Jesus Christ on Easter day.* Then make again the sign of the cross and blow on the patient's eye. Instruct them to say three *Paters* and three *Aves*. In the name of the Father, and of the Son, and of the Holy Spirit.

AGAINST TOOTHACHE

Write these words and wear them hung around the neck: *Stragiles falcesque dentate dentium dolarum persanate.*

DIVINATION BY SIEVE

When one wishes to discover a secret, place a sieve or strainer between the two points of a pair of shears. Then two people each put the middle finger of their left hands under the handle of the shears where the sieve is attached. Then raise it in the air and state what you wish to know, saying: *O sieve, you will turn if it is N who has such and such thing*, then say: *Dies Mies Jeschet Benedœdet, Dowima Enîtamaü.*

If the person named is guilty, the sieve wobbles, turns and falls; if not, begin anew with another name.

FOR BURNS

Our Holy Father goes on His way, and comes across a child who cries: *Father, what has this child? He is fallen in burning coals.* Take some pork breast, and three faggots, and the fire will go out.

FOR EPILEPSY

Exhale into the right ear of the one who has had an epileptic fit saying these words: *Gaspar fert myrrham, thus Melchior, Baltazar aurum.* The patient should recover immediately, and to heal utterly from the condition, it is necessary to take three iron nails the length of his little finger and hammer them into the place he suffered his first fit whilst saying over each the name of the patient.

AGAINST FOXES

Say three times a week: *In the name of the Father* ✠ *and of the Son* ✠ *and of the Holy Spirit,* ✠ *Dog foxes and vixens, I conjure you, in the name of the most Blessed and Holy, as Our Holy Lady was with child, may you neither take nor kill any of my birds or flock, be they cocks, hens or chicks, neither to eat their nests, nor suck their blood, nor break their eggs, nor do any harm to them,* etc.

AGAINST WOLVES

Recíte the same Orison three times a week, saying: *In the name of the Father* ✝ *and of the Son* ✝ *and of the Holy Spirít,* ✝ *wolves and she-wolves, I conjure you, in the name of the most Blessed and Holy, as Our Lady was with child, may you neíther take nor kill any of my birds, flock or herd, be they bulls, cows, calves, rams, ewes, lambs or goats, and all kinds of birds ... etc.*

TO BE HARD

Wríte the following words in your own blood on two pieces of paper: *Ranuc* ✝ *Malin* ✝ *Fora consummatum est, in te confedo, Satana* ✝. Swallow one and wear the other around your neck.

NOTES TO CROSSED KEYS

1 This is similar to the operation we find in *The Red Dragon* which uses a forked stick capped with magnetised iron ferrules. In *The Red Dragon* the magician presents a duplicate wand for the fitting of the ferrules, whereas *The Black Dragon* suggests that you do the work yourself or watch over the process. There would be advantage in using a lodestone and magnetising the wand. The wand in *The Black Dragon* seems reminiscent of the stang of Traditional Craft as popularised by Robert Cochrane and an agricultural tool or perhaps a distaff, rather than a derivation of the dowsing rod.

2 Francois Collet is unknown to history, though *collet* is a snare or noose in French, and this may be a green language pun directing us to be aware of such traps. It may even derive from *colporteurs* the peddlers who sold the Bibliothèque Bleue editions. The spells and counterspells of the second section are in fact taken verbatim from *Honorius*.

3 This pentacle is also found in the *Key of Solomon.*

4 In *Honorius* this reads *Fadal, Nastraché*, rather than the one name with the Hebraic *-el* ending given here.

5 In *Honorius* these are two distinct spirits Passiel and Rosus. The author here has confused *the named one* to refer to *Passiel Rosusr* when it should be read with the sense *Send me presently before this circle, N Passiel, Rosus...* This error has crept in because of the naming of *Fadal Nastrachel* in the *Conjuration of the King of the South.*

6 Figure 2 shows Emperor Lucifer from *The Red Dragon*, though obviously from a corrupted version. Compare the seal we have corrected with this original from *The Black Dragon*:

7 For those who believe that the role of the clerical underground has been overplayed, this is clear evidence that those performing ritual magic were often priests.

8 The instruction is the same in the *Grimorium Verum* which gives more detail on the nature of this spirit. We may conjecture that the stone is bloodstone (heliotrope) and that at some time in the history of the grimoire this has been elided.

9 This contains the Frimost wand sigil, reversed.

10 Shows Astaroth from the *Red Dragon* with tear in eye and bubble of stinking breath again, obviously from a corrupted version reproduced here. This poisoned breath is the malign attribute we also find in the *Goetia* for the demonised goddess who was and is Astarte.

11 Again a hopelessly mangled Silcharde sigil, replaced and reproduced below for comparison. *Honorius* also names him
Acham, a corruption of the biblical Cham: for more on this
see *Abominations*.

12 A corruption of *Eloi Eloi Lama Sabachthani*, spoken by Jesus
on the Cross and rendered in the English as: *My God, My
God, why have you forsaken me.*

13 Though labelled Bechard (also Bechaud), it shows a reversed Surgat sigil. We have reproduced the *Black Dragon*
version below. As the Bechaud sigil is to be written on the
knife in *Verum* and the text concerns wounds we have corrected the seal to reflect this.

14 Figure 7 is indeed Guland, but again mirrored and incomplete. We have corrected the seal in the text and appended the original here. Our choice has been to leave the seals mirrored as ît appears from the complete grimoire that they were meant to be seen 'correctly' in the magic mirror.

15 Recall the warning not to give anything from your own body. Some versions of *Honorius* suggest a fox hair, which is a suitably mercurial substitute. There are further implications here for operations of malefica.

16 Figure 8 shows Bechard rather than Surgat with the sigil fragmented and more reminiscent of the *Verum* seals for L:B:A. We have revised and the original is reproduced here.

THE SECOND PART

17 These forms of chimney/hearth spells are a staple of European witchcraft. For their origins in the hearth magic of ancient Greece and Rome, see *Geosophia* volume II: *Familiar and Unfamiliar Spirits*.

18 Clockwise/deosil.

19 A looking glass, explaining the earlier inversions and with much lore not found in other grimoire sources.

20 June 23rd Summer Solstice and birth of John the Baptist, a date for warding off evil, often with fires. Other plants to be picked on this date in folklore include St John's Wort and Calendula.

21 *Vinca Minor*, a specimen of which we found when walking the day we worked on this page. Periwinkle is a pretty indigo pentagonal flower; *vinca* means to bind, and it spreads rapidly, suggestive of its magical use. Medicinally it enhances blood circulation and aids in cardiovascular diseases.

22 Compare this folk practice to that of the use of bilongos in Palo Mayombe. See *The Garden of Blood and Bones*, Nicholaj de Mattos Frisvold.

23 An essential of magic. See also the *Black Pullet* for the most famous example.

24 This can be done by hand, with an aspergillum or the *Grimorium Verum*'s bound sprigs of mint, marjoram and rosemary.

25 As per the introduction, blackthorn or a new nail, though here it means an iron one as iron is the traditional anti-magic countermeasure. See also fey/fairy lore.

26 It may be that the original spell was performed over an open fire with the toad suspended from a tripod made of these woods.

27 Presumably boxwood. The cross here is reminiscent of crossing the tibia to prevent a spirit walking.

THE THIRD PART

28 Perhaps a misreading of Pliny's *red bramble frog* in his *Natural History*? This also references toadbone lore, which is prevalent across European witchcraft, see Andrew Chumbley's essay *The Leaper Between*.

29 *Thirty six illnesses* suggests the astrological and demonic provenance of disease which we find in the *Testament of Solomon*. Curiously enough the modern insurance industry still lists 36 critical illnesses though not in relation to the ill-starred heavens.

30 Saint Eloy, also Eligius, is the patron saint of horses, blacksmiths and goldsmiths.

31 *This is the wood of the cross on which hung the Saviour of the world.*

32 Figure 11. Again an *Honorius/Verum* form, but surmounted by cross and crescents rather than the Sun, Moon and six pointed star of the original.

33 Willow is traditionally used to drive away snakes, given its sympathies with water. The soaked paper may be a remembrance of spells where the words are washed off the paper and then given to a patient to drink. For alum (alumen) see Pliny, *Natural History* chapter 52 book 35.

34 This is the L:B:S of *Le Livre des Esperitz* rather than the L:B:A of the *Grimorium Verum*.

35 *Telescopus Fallax*, the European Cat Snake is suggested; it may point to their appearance as Holy Snakes of the Virgin Mary which annually congregate on Kefalonia (August 5–15th). Though it may simply be a banded snake, which at a stretch could imply the European Adder.

36 St Peter's Eve is June 28th.

37 Devil's Bit, literally Devil's Bite due to the truncated root stock supposedly bitten off to prevent the horned one sweating at the threat of Judgment Day. What better root to stop a gambler sweating at the card table! The plant, *Scabiosa succisa* was used as a cure for scabies and the plague.

38 *It is finished.* The last words of Christ, *John* 19:30.

THE FOURTH PART

39 *Dragne, Dragne:* unknown meaning, perhaps from or related to *drageonner*, to shoot forth suckers; *drageon*, a sucker; and *dragon*, a dragon.

THE ENCHIRIDION OF POPE LEO III

1 Butterfly: a word play on Pape Leon/Papillon.

2 The central banner should read MKBI in Hebrew, that is, Maccabee. The letters around it read MI KMKH BALM IHVH: *Who is there amongst thee strong as Jehovah?* (*Exodus* 15:11). This derives from the sign given to Judas Machabeus by an Angel prior to his victory over Antiochus Epiphanes. See Agrippa, *Three Books of Occult Philosophy* chapter XXXI and the accompanying notes by Donald Tyson.

3 Asmodeus/Asmoday in the grimoire tradition. See *The Book of Tobit.*

4 The pentagram here represents the five wounds of Christ.
The letters around it are corrupted Greek and should
read ygieia, that is, health. Agrippa in *Three Books of Occult
Philosophy* chapter XXXI, attributes the symbol to Antiochus
Soter. His source in turn is Lucian's *A Slip of the Tongue in
Greeting*, an essay on the Pythagorean pentagram where
he relates that when Antiochus Soter was about to en-
gage the Galatians, he dreamed of Alexander who told him
to give his army the password *Health* before the battle in
which he was victorious. The name and symbol have been
conflated by Agrippa.

5 *Deo Duce Comite Ferro* means: *God as my guide, my companion a
sword*. Found also in the Martial talisman Against all Perils
in the *Key of Solomon*. Though not present in all MSS, it
is reproduced in *The Veritable Key* (Skinner/Rankine). Also
famously it is the magical motto of MacGregor Mathers.

6 Presumably a long barrow or tumulus.

7 Emperor Constantine dreamt of the Chi Rho symbol (⚹),
the first two letters in Greek of Christ, before his battle
with Maxentius and his army bore it with them, either
emblazoned on their shields or as a standard, leading them
to victory. A further embroidered version supplied by
Eusebius in his posthumous *On the life of Constantine* has a
miraculous cross appear in the sky with the words *In this
conquer* seen by the entire army and Christ himself come

to Constantine in a dream with the symbol. Building on Greek ideas the X is seen as the crossing of the solar ecliptic and the celestial equator, but the version presented here is more like a memento mori of crossed tibia. The sash is part of the labarum and perhaps in this rendering suggestive of the priest's stole.

Of more note to grimoire magicians is the previously uncommented similarity between the Chi Rho symbol and the signature of Lucifuge Rofocale in *The Red Dragon*, which is clearly an inversion of the sign set between *N N*. See the illustration below:

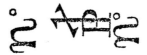

8 Compare with For lifting any spell & summoning the person who has caused harm, page 37 in *The Black Dragon*.

9 See *Black Dragon* note 30 above.

DEDICATIO

He who knows, and knows that he knows, is a wise man. Listen to him! He who knows, and does not know that he knows, is asleep. Awaken him! He who does not know, and knows that he does not know, wants to learn. Teach him! He who does not know, and does not know that he does not know, is a fool. Shun him!

To this work I give a dual dedication:

To my father, Don, who has remained my best and most loyal friend, my greatest teacher, the rock upon whom I lean, who never lost faith in me and who saw my potential when all others had written me off as a life sentence waiting to happen. Who gave all he had, then everything he didn't as well. He whom is the living image of his own father and embodies all he stood for.

To Silvia, Nefertari, who met me two days before my surrender to Federal Prison, who ignored the warnings of her friends and the media and remained by my side, whose kindness, love and beauty kept me grounded as I walked through the valley of death. To Silvia, who looked into the eyes of a demon far more deadly than those about whom he now writes, reached into the abyss that was his soul, and taught him love and friendship. To Silvia, whose unnatural eyes inspire a man to move mountains, and *for whom the Light shines.*

Gratias Vobis Ago:

To HE; to El Indio, my right hand, my mighty fist and the hammer of the gods; to Aset, my protector; Anpu, my initiator; and to Asar, Heru and Seth; to my teachers, Gustavo Colon, Carlo Gambino, Abramelin, Alex Delgado, Salvatore Lucania, Ramesses the Great, Vlad Tepes, Aleister Crowley, Master Sun, Nicolo Machiavelli, H.C. Agrippa and those whose names ought not to be spake; to the needles in the haystack, the few who outweigh the many: Fraters 13, Arcangel, Chino, DB, Papo, Apache, A tiro, Lalo, and to Sorors Fire and Justice. While for the masses, love has to contempt turned, you few are greatly missed, you who are the physical embodiment of our father's vision, and are missed tremendously.

The present translations were made with recourse to various editions of both grimoires,
notably the Bussière and Belfond editions of
Le Veritable Dragon Noir, the reproduction of the
1660 edition of *L'Enchiridion du Pape Léon* published by Editions Bussière, the reproduction
of the 1848 edition published by Belfond, and
that published by H. Durville in two volumes:
Oraisons et Secrets & *Pentacles Protecteurs*.